The
Education
Center®

The MAILBOX
IDEA MAGAZINE FOR TEACHERS®

2009–2010 YEARBOOK

The Education Center, Inc.
Greensboro, North Carolina

The Mailbox® 2009–2010 Preschool Yearbook

Managing Editor, *The Mailbox* Magazine: Kimberly Brugger-Murphy

Editorial Team: Becky S. Andrews, Diane Badden, Kimberley Bruck, Karen A. Brudnak, Pam Crane, Sarah Foreman, Pierce Foster, Margaret Freed (COVER ARTIST), Tazmen Hansen, Marsha Heim, Lori Z. Henry, Kitty Lowrance, Brenda Miner, Jennifer Nunn, Tina Petersen, Gary Phillips (COVER ARTIST), Mark Rainey, Greg D. Rieves, Hope Rodgers, Rebecca Saunders, Donna K. Teal, Rachael Traylor, Sharon M. Tresino, Zane Williard

ISBN10 1-56234-955-4
ISBN13 978-1-56234-955-4
ISSN 1088-5536

Printed in the United States of America.

The Education Center, Inc.
P.O. Box 9753
Greensboro, NC 27429-0753

Look for *The Mailbox® 2010–2011 Preschool Yearbook* in the summer of 2011. The Education Center, Inc., is the publisher of *The Mailbox*®, *Teacher's Helper*®, and *Learning*® magazines, as well as other fine products. Look for these wherever quality teacher materials are sold, call 1-800-714-7991, or visit www.themailbox.com.

RRDWI061022353

Contents

Arts & Crafts for Little Hands

Arts & Crafts for Little Hands

Apple Basket

To make this cute craft, cut a supply of 2" x 3" rectangles from two contrasting shades of brown construction paper. Next, glue the rectangles to a sheet of construction paper in a checkerboard pattern. Then glue apple cutouts and a worm cutout to the project as shown.

Brigitte Dade
Helping Hands Preschool
Medina, OH

Scribble and Paint

This lovely process art has a stained glass effect! To prepare, use food coloring to tint several containers of white corn syrup. Next, use a black crayon to scribble on a sheet of white construction paper. Then use small paintbrushes to paint the resulting shapes and spaces with the syrup. Allow several days for the project to dry.

adapted from an idea by Karla Broad
Our Savior Preschool
Naples, FL

Colorful Swirls

Here's a terrific project youngsters are sure to enjoy! In advance, fill a dishpan or other shallow container with water and then use a food grater to grate an assortment of colorful chalk onto the water. Gently pull a sheet of construction paper across the surface of the water to create a colorful design.

Sandy Barker
ECFE/South Washington County School District
Cottage Grove, MN

Photo Holder

This project makes an adorable Grandparents Day gift or a special beginning-of-the-year memento! Paint a scrap wood block or one purchased from a local craft store. After the paint dries, decorate the block with craft foam shapes; then hot-glue two jumbo paper clips to the back as shown. (Hot glue gun is for teacher use.) Finally, slide a photograph into the clips.

Amy Durrwachter
Kirkwood Early Childhood Center
Kirkwood, MO

Arts & Crafts for Little Hands

Faux Autumn Leaf

To make a leaf, use fall-colored crayons to color a brown paper bag leaf cutout. Then sponge-paint the entire surface of the leaf with thinned brown paint. After the paint is dry, tightly crumple the leaf and then straighten it out. The result is an authentic-looking autumn leaf with a veined effect!

Elizabeth Cook
Clayton, MO

Painted Flames

Squeeze thin lines of red and yellow paint onto a sheet of white construction paper. Then use a cotton ball to gently stroke the paint upward, blending the colors so the paint resembles flames. To complete the project, press a simple fire truck cutout onto the wet paint. The fire truck is rushing to put out the flames!

Melinda Riley
Faith Christian Preschool
Lafayette, IN

Awesome Owl

Brush glue on a brown disposable paper plate; then press feathers on the glue. Continue until the plate is covered with feathers. Glue cupcake liners (eyes) to the plate; then glue a jumbo wiggle eye to each liner. To complete the owl, cut a beak and two feet from construction paper scraps and glue them in place.

Deanne Gigante
Lamb School
Houston, TX

Festive Decoration

This project makes a perfect Thanksgiving centerpiece! To begin, staple silk leaves around the rim of a heavyweight paper plate. To make a pilgrim hat, glue a black paper circle to the plate; then glue to the circle a black paper cylinder decorated with a yellow strip. To make the headband, tape colorful craft feathers to a paper cylinder; then glue the headband to the plate. Finally, glue other fall items, such as Indian corn and small gourds, to the project.

Patti Wolf
Kids Cozy Corners
Hartford, WI

Arts & Crafts for Little Hands

Gingerbread Head

This cute craft is so easy to make it's perfect for even the youngest preschooler! To make one, paint a paper plate brown. Next, glue craft foam shapes to the plate to create facial details. Then glue a length of rick-rack and a bow to the project.

Phyllis Prestridge
West Amory Elementary
Amory, MS

Footprint Snowflake

This one-of-a-kind snowflake will never melt! To make one, press the bottom of your foot in white paint and then press it onto a large tagboard square. Repeat the process, making more footprints and arranging them as shown. To complete the snowflake, draw a face on a white construction paper circle; then glue the circle to the tagboard. Add additional details as desired.

Bobbi Kolacki
Bright Beginnings Preschool
Loganville, GA

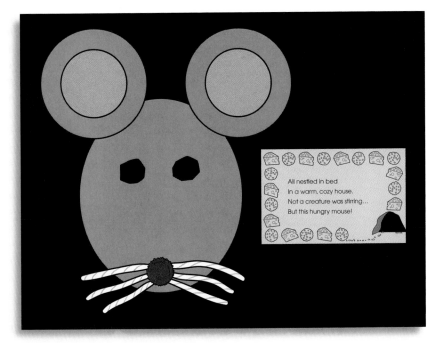

Who's Awake?

To prepare, cut out two medium-size gray construction paper circles (ears), two small pink construction paper circles (inner ears), and a large gray construction paper oval (head). To make this adorable mouse, simply glue the pieces to a sheet of construction paper as shown. Then add a red pom-pom nose, black eye cutouts, and yarn whiskers. Finally, attach a copy of the poem from page 19 to the project.

Joyce Wilson
Trophy Club, TX

Mischievous Cats

Cats just love to climb Christmas trees! To make this cute holiday art, glue a large tree cutout to a 12" x 18" sheet of construction paper. Next, decorate the tree with collage materials, such as colorful sticky dots, sequins, holiday-related craft foam shapes, and ribbon. Then color and cut out copies of the cat patterns on page 20 and glue them to the project so it looks like they are climbing up the tree. Those curious little cats!

Diane Mascola
Stanton Learning Center
Stanton, NJ

Arts & Crafts for Little Hands

Warm Heart

To make this sweet craft, glue two construction paper mittens to a large heart cutout. Next, glue cotton batting to each mitten so the cotton resembles a cuff. Then decorate the mittens with seasonal stickers to make a matching pair. Finally, label the project "Warm Hands, Warm Heart."

Jennie Jensen
Clarence, IA

Process Art

Roll a Rainbow

Draw a rainbow on a sheet of paper. Dip the wheels of a toy vehicle in paint; then roll the vehicle along one arc, adding more paint to the wheels as needed. Continue with other vehicles and colors of paint for each remaining arc. To complete the project, glue a black pot cutout to one end of the rainbow. Then add gold glitter to the top of the pot so it resembles a pot of gold.

JoAnn Weigand
Haddonfield Methodist Church Nursery School
Haddonfield, NJ

Shimmering Shamrock

Use green food coloring to tint corn syrup; then mix a generous amount of glitter into the syrup. To make a shamrock, glue three white construction paper hearts to a sheet of paper as shown. Then glue a green paper strip to the shamrock to make a stem. Finally, brush a thick layer of the mixture onto the shamrock. Allow several days for the project to dry.

adapted from an idea by Monica Pyka
Brookfield Elementary
Brookfield, WI

Dandy Designs

This process art results in unique textured designs! To prepare, hot-glue to a cardboard tube assorted craft materials, such as buttons, uncooked pasta, crumpled paper, and yarn. To make a print, roll the tube in a shallow container of paint and then roll it on a sheet of paper. Continue in the same way, overlapping the designs if desired.

Staci McQuain
Echo, OR

Process Art

Arts & Crafts for Little Hands

Stained Glass

Paint a sheet of waxed paper with diluted glue, making sure the paper is quite wet. Next, press pieces of colorful tissue paper on the glue. Then paint a second sheet of waxed paper with diluted glue and press it painted-side down on the decorated paper. These projects look lovely displayed on a window.

Patricia Farley
Just for Kids
Sparta, WI

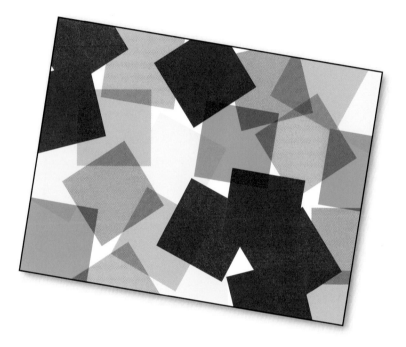

Tie-Dye Butterfly

To make a butterfly, put a generous amount of nonmentholated shaving cream on a tray. Use eyedroppers to drip different colors of diluted paint onto the shaving cream; then blend the colors into the shaving cream using a craft stick. Next, press a butterfly cutout on the shaving cream; then lift the paper from the tray. Finally, use the side of the craft stick to gently remove the excess shaving cream from the paper.

Misty Moesser
North Park Elementary
North Logan, UT

Just Hatched

To make this cute craft, glue brown crinkle shreds to a disposable bowl. Next, glue yellow craft feathers, two paper dots (eyes), and an orange construction paper triangle (beak) to a large yellow pom-pom (chick); then glue the chick in a plastic egg half. To complete the craft, glue the egg to the crinkle shreds.

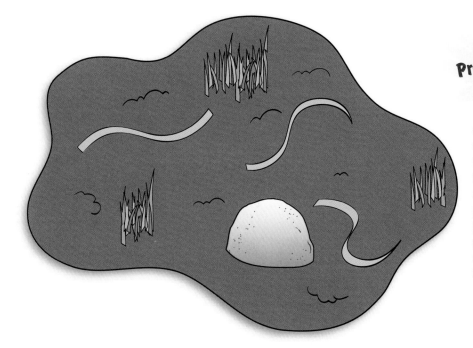

Process Art

Mud Puddle

To prepare, blend oatmeal into equal amounts of brown paint and glue to create a thick mudlike texture. To make a mud puddle, fingerpaint a thick layer of the mixture onto a sheet of brown paper. Then embellish the mud puddle by pressing items—such as grass, rocks, and cut rubber bands (worms)—in it. When the paint is dry, trim around the puddle.

Arts & Crafts for Little Hands

One-of-a-Kind Bee

Here's an adorable bee craft! To make one, paint your palm and fingers with black and yellow stripes as shown; then press your hand onto a sheet of paper, keeping your fingers together. Glue a black paper circle (head) and a pair of construction paper wings to the print. To complete the bee, glue hole-punch dots (eyes) to the head and draw two antennae; then decorate the page as desired.

Kathy Siegel
Franklin First United Methodist Preschool
Franklin, TN

 Process Art

Waffle Designs

To create unique and colorful artwork, dip a frozen waffle in paint and then press it onto a sheet of paper, adding more paint to the waffle as needed. Continue with other frozen waffles and colors of paint, overlapping the prints as desired.

Joyce Wilson
Trophy Club, TX

Simple Seagull

Paint the back of a paper plate dark gray. Cut the plate, as shown, to make the seagull's head, wings, and body. On the front of the plate, draw two eyes on the head; then glue construction paper legs, feet, and a beak in place. Finally, fold the wings forward as shown.

Elizabeth Cook
St. Louis, MO

Process Art ## Holiday Fireworks

Use tinsel to create a shiny fireworks display! Simply cut colorful rope tinsel into small pieces. Then glue the pieces to a sheet of black paper. Finally, decorate the paper with foil stars.

Keely Peasner
Liberty Ridge Head Start
Bonney, WA

Cozy Campfire

To make this cozy campfire, tear strips of brown construction paper (logs) and glue them to a sheet of black paper. Next, press your hand in orange paint and then onto the paper above the logs (flames). Repeat this step several times. Finally, glue a moon cutout to the page and attach star stickers.

Janet Boyce
Cokato, MN

Process Art

Sandy Seashore

This process art will tickle your fingertips! To prepare, mix a generous amount of sand into light brown paint. Also lightly swirl together green paint and blue paint. To make the seashore, fingerpaint a thick layer of the sandy mixture near the top of a sheet of white construction paper. Then finger-paint the rest of the paper with the blue and green paint to make the ocean. When the paint is dry, use glue to make a few wave lines in the ocean and then sprinkle glitter over the glue so it resembles white-caps.

Ada Goren
Winston-Salem, NC

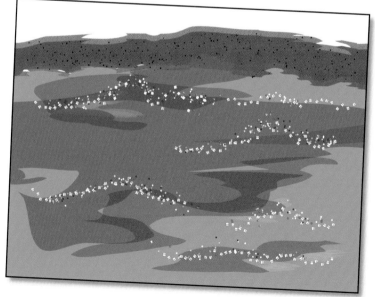

All nestled in bed

In a warm, cozy house.

Not a creature was stirring…

But this hungry mouse!

TEC41046

All nestled in bed

In a warm, cozy house.

Not a creature was stirring…

But this hungry mouse!

TEC41046

Cat Patterns

Use with "Mischievous Cats" on page 11.

TEC41046

TEC41046

TEC41046

BUSY HANDS

Busy Hands

Fine-Motor Explorations for the Season

School Tool Patterns

Outline school supplies on strips of paper to make simple AB patterns. Place the strips at a table along with the supplies. A child chooses a strip and places the objects on the strip to make the pattern.

Tricia Brown, Bowling Green, KY

Letters and Numbers

Fill a box with paper shreds; then tuck into the shreds an assortment of letter and number cookie cutters (or letter and number cards). Place two containers, each labeled with letters or numbers, next to the box. A youngster digs through the shreds and puts each cookie cutter she finds in its corresponding container.

Tricia Brown

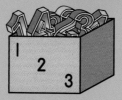

I Spy Collage

Attach a large sheet of bulletin board paper to a tabletop. Each child visits the table and glues on the paper a photo of himself, along with a variety of colorful craft items. Hang the resulting collage on a wall and use it to play I Spy, encouraging youngsters to search for specific classmates.

Picture-Perfect

Laminate large skin-toned circle cutouts and place them at a center along with colorful play dough, rolling pins, and scissors. A student shapes and cuts the dough to make facial features and hair and places the pieces on a circle to create a likeness of herself.

Blue

Pink

Green

School Bus Driver

Place student photos at several mock bus stops around the classroom. Provide a tagboard school bus cutout with a resealable plastic bag attached to the back. A youngster pretends to drive the school bus to each bus stop, picking up students (placing the photos in the bag) along the way.

Tricia Brown, Bowling Green, KY

Busy Hands

Fine-Motor Explorations for the Season

ideas contributed by Tricia Kylene Brown, Bowling Green, KY

Mini Pumpkin Patch

Fill your sensory table with Easter grass or paper shreds; then hide miniature pumpkins in the table. Place a plastic pumpkin pail nearby. A child digs through the makeshift pumpkin patch and puts each pumpkin she finds in the pail.

Monster Makeover

Youngsters have fun creating silly monster characters! Provide tagboard shapes and an assortment of craft items. A child arranges the shapes as desired; then he places craft items on the shapes to add facial features and other details to his silly monster.

SUPERSIMPLE MURAL

Make a supersize treat bag from colorful bulletin board paper and place it at a table along with a supply of sponges cut into shapes and shallow pans of paint. Have youngsters make sponge prints on the bag so the prints resemble candy. When the paint is dry, display the paper on a wall.

LEAFY COLLAGE

Place an oversize poster board leaf cutout at a table along with a collection of colorful fall leaves and glue. Each student visits the center and glues leaves to the cutout.

HAPPY HARVEST

The crops are ready to harvest! Place harvest food cutouts (or plastic harvest foods) around your classroom and provide a childsize basket. A youngster carries the basket around the room, "harvesting" the foods along the way.

Fine-Motor Explorations for the Season

PATCHWORK MITTEN

Place an oversize mitten cutout at a table along with paper scraps from gift wrap, scrapbook paper, and construction paper. Youngsters cut or tear paper scraps and glue them to the mitten. Then students glue cotton balls to the mitten to make a cuff. When the glue is dry, trim any excess paper from the edges of the mitten.

Siobhan Mumford, Early Childhood Center, Cranston, RI

WHIMSICAL WREATH

Provide a tagboard wreath cutout along with large colorful pom-poms and seasonal craft foam or die-cut shapes. A child arranges the items on the cutout to create a unique holiday wreath.

Tricia Brown, Bowling Green, KY

Sweet Gingerbread House

Draw on brown poster board a large house with simple details. Cut out the house and place it at a table along with colorful pom-poms, craft foam shapes, candy stickers, and glue. Students decorate the cutout so it resembles a gingerbread house.

Pam Vannatta, Kids N Kapers Daycare, Lexington, KY

Dazzling Holiday Tree

Place a large poster board tree outline at a table with a supply of self-adhesive gift bows. Have youngsters attach bows inside the outline. If desired, glue cinnamon sticks to the tree trunk.

Anne Marie Thomas, Augusta Preparatory Day School, Martinez, GA

Frosty Fun

Draw a snowy landscape on a length of blue construction paper. Then place the paper on your floor with a container of cotton balls (snowballs). A child places snowballs on the paper in groups of three to make oodles of snowmen.

ideas contributed by Tricia Brown, Bowling Green, KY

LIONS AND LAMBS

Fill your sensory table with paper shreds; then hide yellow and white pom-poms in the shreds to represent lions and lambs, respectively. Provide two containers. A youngster searches for the lions and lambs and then sorts them into the containers.

MIX-AND-MATCH VALENTINES

Cut leftover valentines in half using the same puzzle cut. Store the pieces in a container. A child assembles card halves with corresponding designs. Then she assembles card halves with different designs to create her own unique valentines.

COLORFUL KITE TAIL

Attach to a wall a large kite cutout with a ribbon tail. Provide a container of colorful spring-style clothespins. A youngster chooses a clothespin and clips it to the kite tail. She continues adding clothespins as desired.

BLOWING IN THE WIND

Tape a sheet of light blue bulletin board paper to a tabletop. Attach a cloud shape to the paper and draw a few motion lines so they resemble wind. Provide a variety of magazines. A child cuts pictures from magazines and glues them to the paper so it appears as though the items are blowing in the wind.

GLUE STICK

LUCKY LEPRECHAUN

Place shamrock cutouts and medium-size, gold-painted rocks (gold nuggets) around your classroom. Also provide a black plastic pot. If desired, provide a plastic holiday-related hat for youngsters to wear. A child carries the pot around the room, collecting shamrocks and gold nuggets along the way.

Busy Hands

Fine-Motor Explorations for the Season

ideas contributed by Lucia Kemp Henry

SPRING FLOWERS

Poke holes in several large plastic containers and place them upside down in your empty water table. Provide silk flowers and a spray bottle filled with water. A youngster pushes a flower stem through the hole in each container. Then she uses the spray bottle to spritz the flowers with water.

BEAUTIFUL BLOSSOMS

Provide a large tree cutout along with a supply of construction paper blossoms and pom-poms. A child arranges blossoms on the tree branches and then puts a pom-pom in the center of each blossom.

Hungry Hen

Attach a simple hen cutout to a sheet of poster board. Provide black and brown stamp pads. Youngsters press their fingers on the ink pads and then make prints (chicken feed) on the poster board for the hungry hen to eat.

Bunny Trail

Attach a large sheet of bulletin board paper to a tabletop and draw a wide path on the paper. A child traces a bunny-shaped cookie cutter or tracer on the path. Next, he uses markers to add fur and facial details to the bunny. Then he glues on a cotton ball tail. Youngsters continue to add bunnies until the path is full.

Hidden Eggs

Fill a large tub with Easter grass or paper shreds; then hide plastic eggs in the tub. Provide a sterilized foam egg carton and a pair of tongs. A youngster searches through the tub to find an egg and then uses the tongs to pick it up and place it in the egg carton.

Busy Hands

Fine-Motor Explorations for the Season

ideas contributed by Ada Goren, Winston-Salem, NC

SPECTACULAR SUNSET

Attach a sheet of light blue bulletin board paper to a tabletop. Set out shallow containers of yellow, orange, and red paint along with a small foam paint roller for each color. A child dips each roller in paint and then rolls it across the paper, overlapping the colors so they resemble a sunset. After each child has a turn, complete the sunset by pressing a large yellow semicircle (sun) in the wet paint.

COLORFUL ICE POPS

Set out a supply of colorful tagboard ice pop shapes along with a container of spring-style clothespins. A youngster chooses an ice pop and then clips two clothespins to the bottom edge so they resemble ice pop sticks.

TROPICAL TREE

Attach a palm tree trunk cutout to a wall. Provide a supply of large green construction paper leaves and scissors. Have each child fringe-cut the edges of a leaf. As each youngster finishes, help him attach his leaf to the top of the tree trunk.

OCEAN SCENERY

Tape a sheet of blue bulletin board paper to a tabletop; then draw a few lines so they resemble ocean waves. Provide a supply of ocean-related stickers (or self-adhesive craft foam shapes) along with crayons or markers. Each student visits the table, peels the backing off desired stickers, and attaches the stickers to the paper. Then she draws details as desired.

GATHERING SEASHELLS

Place medium-size seashells (or seashell cutouts) around your classroom and provide a plastic sand pail. A youngster carries the pail around the room, collecting seashells along the way.

Mouse's Glitter Crayons

Note to the teacher: Have each student color each crayon a different color. Then encourage her to dab glue on the tip of each crayon, in turn, and sprinkle clear glitter over the glue.

Note to the teacher: For fine-motor practice, have each child cut out the bats on a copy of this page and then glue the bats to the cave.

©The Mailbox® • TEC41045 • Oct./Nov. 2009

THE MAILBOX **35**

Cozy Stocking

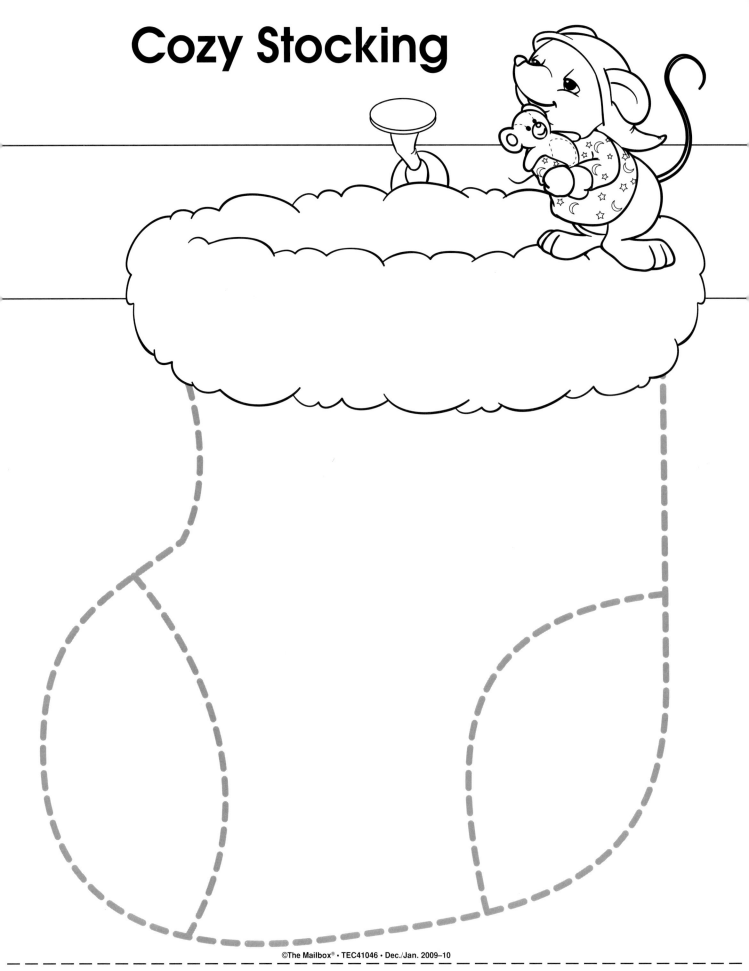

Note to the teacher: Have each youngster trace the stocking on a copy of this page and then color the page. Encourage her to crumple white tissue paper squares and glue them to the page to fill in the stocking cuff.

Note to the teacher: Have each child color a copy of the page. Then have her crumple and glue yellow tissue paper squares above the pot to represent gold.

Mole's Garden

©The Mailbox® • TEC41048 • April/May 2010

Note to the teacher: Have students tear brown construction paper scraps into small pieces (seeds) and glue them to the garden.

CIRCLE TIME

Circle Time

Classroom Sort

Place in a bag several items from different areas of the room, such as a paintbrush and watercolors from the art area and books and pillows from the reading area. Place hoops on the floor and label them to match the areas represented by the items. Ask a volunteer to pick an item from the bag. Have students identify the item and name ways to use it. Then have a child place the item in the appropriate hoop. Continue with each remaining item. Then have youngsters help you place the items where they belong.

adapted from an idea by Tricia Brown
Bowling Green, KY

Art Center

If Your Name Is...

Students learn classmates' names with this activity! Place in a gift bag a name card for each child. Invite a volunteer to pick a card. Announce the name on the card; then lead the group in singing the song shown, encouraging the child who was named to stand up. After the third line of the song, have everyone stand and cheer. Then prompt students to sit quickly and sing the final line.

(sung to the tune of "If You're Happy and You Know It")

If you're [child's name] and you know it, please stand up!
If you're [child's name] and you know it, please stand up!
We're so glad that [child's name]'s here. Let's all stand and give a cheer!
If you're [child's name] and you know it, please stand up!

Creedence Cathey
Conroe, TX

Addi

So Many Feelings

In advance, make a class supply of emotion stick puppets like the ones shown. (See cards on page 57.) Provide each student with a puppet. Lead youngsters in singing the song shown, encouraging each child with a happy puppet to hold it in the air at the appropriate time. Then have each child in the group act out the feeling. Repeat the song several times, substituting the name of a different feeling until all the puppets have been used.

(sung to the tune of "Where Is Thumbkin?")

Where is [happy]?
Where is [happy]?
Here I am.
Here I am.
I am very [happy].
I am very [happy].
Yes, I am.
Yes, I am.

Kilynda Moore, Kingswood Playschool, Rural Hall, NC

Class Stars

Cut a square hole in a large box. Add details so the box resembles a television; then tape black paper over the hole to create a flap. While a student covers her eyes, encourage another child to hide inside the mock TV. Then prompt the first student to uncover her eyes. Encourage her to guess which classmate is hidden, providing help as needed. After the child's name is revealed, lead youngsters in the chant shown. Lift the flap at the end of the chant to reveal the star of the show. The star then becomes the guesser.

Our class is filled with stars, you know.
Turn on the TV.
It's the [child's name] show!

Denise Manly
Ottawa County Early Childhood Center
Oak Harbor, OH

Circle Time

Pumpkin Nose

Mount on a wall a poster board jack-o'-lantern, minus a nose. Place several tagboard shapes in a pumpkin pail. To begin, invite a child to choose a shape from the pail; then have the group identify the shape. Attach Sticky-Tac to the shape. Next, have the child cover his eyes with a sleep mask. Encourage him to stick the nose on the pumpkin; then have him remove the mask to see where he placed the nose. Repeat the process with each remaining shape.

Lenny D. Grozier
Bringhamton, NY

Colorful Leaves

Give each child a leaf cutout in a fall color. Then have youngsters walk in a circle as you lead them in singing the song shown. After singing the last line, have students stop walking; then prompt each child with the appropriate leaf to let it float to the floor. Repeat the song with each remaining leaf color. After all the leaves have fallen, invite little ones to jump in the leaf pile!

(sung to the tune of "Are You Sleeping?")

We love fall leaves.
We love fall leaves.
Yes we do!
Yes we do!
Watch the pretty [red] leaves,
Watch the pretty [red] leaves
Falling down to the ground.

Jenny Baker
South Penn Elementary
Cumberland, MD

Who Stole the Pumpkin?

Here's a seasonal twist on a traditional rhyme! Purchase pumpkin-flavored treats, such as pumpkin cookies, and hide them from view. Then place on the floor a personalized pumpkin cutout for each child (pattern on page 58). Prompt a child to pick a pumpkin and hand it to you. Then follow the script below. After each child's pumpkin has been picked, admit that you stole the pumpkin and used it to make special treats. Reveal the pumpkin treats and give one to each child. What fun!

Teacher: [Child's name] stole the pumpkin from the pumpkin patch.
Child: Who, me?
Teacher: Yes, you!
Child: Couldn't be!
Teacher: Then who?

Janna Meister
Parkwood Weekday Early Education Center
Jacksonville, FL

Feathery Letter Match

Attach a simple turkey body cutout to a wall. Then label pairs of construction paper feathers with matching letters and place the feathers on the floor. Invite a volunteer to choose a feather and then look for its match. When he finds the matching feather, prompt students to jump up and strut around the room while gobbling like turkeys. Then help the child attach both feathers to the turkey. Repeat the process for each remaining pair of feathers.

adapted from an idea by Andrea Singleton
Waynesville Elementary
Waynesville, OH

Circle Time

I Spy Pizza

Cut a large red circle into wedges and decorate each wedge with different craft materials to make unique pizza slices. Place the slices in a clean pizza box or on a pan. Next, play a game of I Spy. Say, for example, "I spy a pizza slice with pumpkin stickers and feathers." Then ask a child to point to the matching slice. If he is correct, have him remove the slice and pretend to take a bite. If he is incorrect, another child takes a turn.

Roxanne LaBell Dearman
Western NC Early Intervention Program for Children Who Are
Deaf or Hard of Hearing, Charlotte, NC

Silly Rhyme Time

Play this nonsense rhyming game with your youngsters! Gently pat your legs in a steady rhythm and say, "Gobble, gobble, pet." Keep up the steady rhythm and encourage a child to name a word (real or nonsense) that rhymes with *pet,* preceding his word with "Gobble, gobble." Allow several more students to take turns. Then begin the game again with a new word.

Laura Wagner
Raleigh, NC

Gobble, gobble, set!

Circle Time

Winter Animals

Discuss with youngsters how different animals survive during the cold winter months. Explain that some frogs bury themselves in mud at the bottom of a pond, some bears sleep in caves, some birds migrate to warmer climates, and some squirrels gather and store nuts. Then recite the rhyme shown, encouraging little ones to act out the animal named. If desired, cover your little frogs with a blanket (mud), invite your bears to "hibernate" under tables (caves), encourage your birds to "fly" to a predetermined area (warmer climate), and have your squirrels gather nut cutouts placed around the room.

Winter is coming.
It's time to prepare.
Get ready, little [animal name],
For the cold winter air!

Laurie Eberli, Just For Kids Preschool
Everett, WA

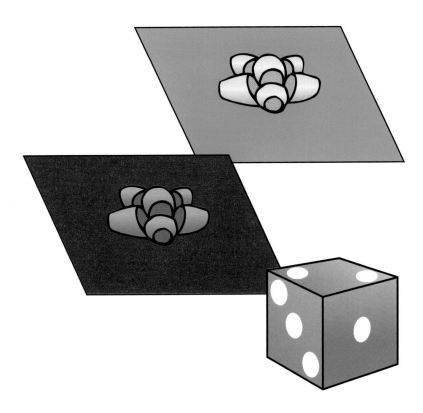

Counting Gifts

To prepare for this activity, attach gift bows to construction paper squares so they resemble gifts. Invite a volunteer to roll a large foam die and then count aloud that number of gifts. Encourage the group to count along. Then have him place the gifts under your class tree (or near a poster board tree cutout). Continue in the same way with different volunteers.

Tricia Kylene Brown
Bowling Green, KY

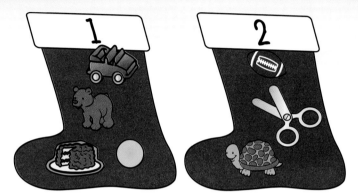

Which Stocking?

Display three stocking cutouts numbered as shown. Store in a cloth sack an assortment of familiar items or pictures of items whose names contain one, two, and three syllables. Ask a child (Santa or Mrs. Claus) to pick an item from the sack and identify its name. Then have her repeat the name and clap the syllables. Finally, have her place the item on the appropriate stocking. Repeat the process with the remaining items.

Kathryn Davenport
Partin Elementary
Oviedo, FL

Colorful Snowman

To prepare, cut from felt a snowman, a blue hat, two black eyes, an orange carrot nose, a red smile, two brown stick arms, and a yellow scarf. Put the snowman on your flannelboard and place the remaining items nearby. To begin, invite a student to place the hat on the snowman's head. Then lead the group in singing the song shown. Continue in the same way with the remaining items, changing the underlined words as appropriate.

(sung to the tune of "Skip to My Lou")

> Snowman with the [blue hat],
> I see you.
> Snowman with the [blue hat],
> I see you.
> Snowman with the [blue hat],
> I see you
> Through my frosty window!

LeeAnn Collins, Sunshine House Preschool, Lansing, MI

Gingerbread Pairs

Make a class supply of pairs of gingerbread man cutouts (pattern on page 59), making sure each pair is distinct. Distribute half of each pair to the class and store the remaining cutouts in a bag. Pick a cutout from the bag and hold it in the air. Then say, "Think, think as fast as you can! Who has the match to this gingerbread man?" The student with the matching gingerbread man holds it in the air. Continue with each remaining gingerbread man.

Tammy Stapley
The Preschool Club
Eugene, OR

Taste-Test Pattern

Cut out several copies of the taste cards on page 59. Have youngsters participate in a taste test with the foods pictured on the cards. Then arrange several cards in a desired pattern and read the pattern aloud. Next, invite volunteers to add cards to the pattern. Repeat the process with different patterns.

Kathleen Carter, Mulberry Elementary
Wilkesboro, NC

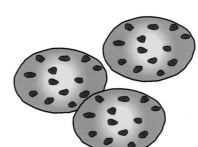

| Salty | Sweet | Salty | Sweet |

Circle Time

Special Delivery

Label several paper strips with directions such as "Reach up high and then touch your toes" and "Jump up and down ten times." Put each strip in an envelope; then place the unsealed envelopes in a tote bag. Give the bag to a volunteer and have her pretend she is a mail carrier. Encourage the mail carrier to call out, "Special delivery for [child's name]!" Then have her deliver an envelope to the child, who removes the strip for you to read aloud. After youngsters complete the directions, have the two students switch places. Continue the activity until the bag is empty.

Eileen Gingras
The Children's School at Deerfield Academy
Deerfield, MA

Searching for Clovers

Place a class supply of four-leaf clover cutouts (patterns on page 60) around the room. Tell your little leprechauns that four-leaf clovers are lucky. Recite the rhyme shown and then encourage each leprechaun to find one clover and bring it back to his seat. Prompt students to pile the clovers together. Then help students count the clovers. That's a lot of luck!

Hello, little leprechauns.
This is your lucky day
For finding four-leaf clovers,
So hurry on your way!

Cherie Durbin
Hickory, NC

Color Cube

Cover each side of a cube-shaped box with a different color of paper. Store an assortment of corresponding objects in a sack. Invite a volunteer to roll the cube; then ask the group to identify the color that lands on top. Next, have the volunteer remove an object from the sack. If the object's color matches the color on the top of the cube, prompt the child to set the item aside. If not, have her put the item back in the sack. Continue the activity until the sack is empty.

adapted from an idea by Karen Smith, Little Tid-Bits, Fresno, CA

Mr. Groundhog

Give each child a brown construction paper groundhog (patterns on page 61). Have him place the groundhog on the floor and pretend it is asleep in its burrow. Then recite the poem shown. If the two underlined words rhyme, instruct each youngster to pretend to have his groundhog wake and peek out of its burrow. If the words do not rhyme, instruct youngsters to keep their groundhogs still. Repeat the activity several times, replacing the underlined words each time.

Mr. Groundhog, fast asleep,
Please wake up and take a peek
When you hear two words that rhyme.
Now listen carefully: [blue], [shoe].

Circle Time

Mail Time!

Set out a mock mailbox and give each youngster a letter card. Recite the rhyme shown, naming one of the letters. Prompt youngsters with the appropriate cards to hold them in the air and then place them in the mailbox. Repeat the activity until each child has mailed his card.

Let's all mail a card today.
Send the *[C]* cards on their way!

adapted from an idea by Barbara Rackley
Kingdom Academy
Sarasota, FL

How Many Tarts?

Make several felt tart cutouts as shown. Help youngsters recite the first few lines of the traditional "Queen of Hearts" nursery rhyme (see below). Then place five tart cutouts on your flannelboard. Tell students that the knave stole three of the tarts. Have a youngster pretend to be the knave, sneak up to the board, and remove three tarts. Prompt students to count the remaining tarts. Repeat the process, having a knave remove a different number of tarts each time.

The Queen of Hearts, she made some tarts
All on a summer's day.
The Knave of Hearts, he stole the tarts
And took them clean away.

Kim Harker, Discovery Express Preschool
Mendon, CT

Circle Time

Little Clouds

Give each child a cloud cutout. Then have two students walk around the circle with their clouds as you lead the group in reciting the first verse of the poem shown. At the end of the verse, have three more students join the first two. Lead the class in counting the clouds to determine the total number. Continue in the same way until all the students have joined the group. Then recite the final verse, encouraging youngsters to perform the movements shown.

[Two] little rain clouds floating by,
Gently moving through the sky.
The clouds were having so much fun,
They invited [three] more clouds to come.

All the rain clouds floating by   *Move in a circle.*
Gathered together in the sky.   *Stop. Extend clouds into the circle.*
They made a great big thunderous sound;   *Stomp your feet.*
Then all the raindrops fell to the ground!   *Sit on the floor.*

adapted from an idea by Susan Pufall
Red Cliff Early Head Start
Bayfield, WI

A Blooming Garden

Die-cut colorful flowers and place them in a decorative bag. Recite the rhyme shown, inserting a child's name. Prompt the child to choose a flower and name its color. Then have the child place the flower on the floor (garden). Continue in the same way, having each remaining child add a flower to the garden.

[Child's name, child's name], quite contrary,
Look at this garden grow!
Won't you add a flower today
And take a seat just so?

Shelley Hoster
Jack & Jill Early Learning Center
Norcross, GA

Counting Raindrops

Place a puddle-shaped cutout on the floor. Store a supply of tagboard raindrops in a bag. Invite a student to take a handful of raindrops and drop them over the puddle. Next, have him count aloud each raindrop that fell in the puddle and each raindrop that fell on the floor. Encourage the group to count along. Finally, ask youngsters to compare the number of raindrops on the puddle to those on the floor.

adapted from an idea by Shelli Hurlocker
Busy Bees Christian Preschool
Kokomo, IN

Dress-Up Sounds

Choose a variety of clothing items with names that begin with different letters. You might use the following items: apron, tie, coat, socks, robe, hat, vest, and boots. Prompt a child to choose and then don an article of clothing. Then encourage the remaining students to identify the name of the clothing and its beginning sound. Continue until all the items have been worn.

Marie E. Cecchini
West Dundee, IL

Rhyme Time

To prepare, place several different items in a basket. Instruct youngsters to pass the basket around the circle as you lead the group in reciting a familiar rhyme. The child holding the basket at the end of the rhyme keeps it in his lap. Announce a word (real or nonsense) that rhymes with one of the items in the basket. Then have the youngster holding the basket find the rhyming object and show it to the group.

Marie E. Cecchini
West Dundee, IL

I Spy Letters

Give each student a copy of page 62 along with eight raindrop cutouts. Sing the song shown, naming one of the letters on the page. Then ask each child to point to the raindrop on the page labeled with the selected letter. After scanning for accuracy, have each student place a raindrop cutout atop the appropriate letter. Repeat the activity with each remaining letter.

(sung to the tune of "Three Blind Mice")

I spy *[R]*, I spy *[R]*
Somewhere on the page,
Somewhere on the page!
Look at the raindrops so carefully;
Look at them closely and you will see
The letter *[R]*, I'm sure you'll agree.
I spy *[R]*, I spy *[R]*.

adapted from an idea by Donna Olp
St. Gregory the Great School
South Euclid, OH

Look, Listen, Match

Cut apart several different greeting cards. Display each card front in your pocket chart and stack the card backs nearby. To begin, have youngsters study the displayed cards. Then take a card back from the stack and read its verse aloud. Next, invite a volunteer to place the verse beside its card front. Continue until all the card halves are matched.

Marie E. Cecchini
West Dundee, IL

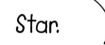

Star.

Which One Rhymes?

Display several objects and lead the group in naming each one. Then announce a real or nonsense word that rhymes with one of the item's names. Ask the group to decide which item's name rhymes with the word; then lead youngsters in saying the word pair. After confirming that the two words rhyme, set the item aside. Continue with each remaining item.

I see Rosalie looking at me!

Who Do You See?

Ask a student to stand in the center of the circle and close his eyes. Help him slowly spin around as you lead the rest of the group in chanting, "[Marcus, Marcus], who do you see?" At the end of the chant, stop the child and direct him to open his eyes and identify the student who is facing him by saying, "I see [Rosalie] looking at me!" Have the two students switch places. Continue until each child has had a turn to spin around or until interest wanes.

Goldie Pollack
Brooklyn, NY

What's in the Bag?

Conceal in a beach-style bag a variety of beach-related items, such as a pair of sunglasses, a flip-flop, a sun hat, a small plastic shovel, a towel, and an empty bottle of sunscreen. Display the bag and tell little ones it is filled with items they would use at the beach. Then give youngsters clues to help them guess one of the items. When the correct item is named, remove it from the bag to confirm the guess; then set the item aside. Continue the activity until the bag is empty.

Ada Goren
Winston-Salem, NC

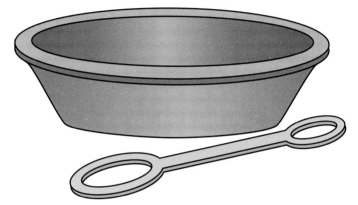

Imaginary Bubbles

Obtain a bubble wand and an empty container for pretend bubble solution. Have youngsters crouch down near the floor. Dip the wand in the container and then wave it in the air. As you wave the wand, encourage little ones to slowly rise onto their tiptoes and pretend to be bubbles floating in the air. After a few moments, chant, "Bubbles, bubbles in the air. Bubbles popping everywhere!" At the end of the chant, have your little bubbles clap their hands as they pretend to burst and then quickly crouch back down. Continue for several more rounds.

adapted from an idea by Janet Boyce
Cokato, MN

You always play nicely with your friends.

Kindness Counts

This cute idea reminds youngsters to use kind words when speaking. To begin the activity, elicit a few examples of kind things to say. Then invite a student to put on a pair of sunglasses adorned with items such as sequins or plastic jewels. Have her face a classmate who is sitting next to her and say, "Fancy sunglasses, yes sirree! Please say something nice to me!" Encourage the classmate to say something nice to the child. Then have the child pass the sunglasses to the classmate. Continue in the same way.

Nicole Liversage
Associazione Culturale Linguistica Educational
Sanremo, Italy

happy

TEC41044

sad

TEC41044

embarrassed

TEC41044

excited

TEC41044

angry

TEC41044

worried

TEC41044

Pumpkin Pattern

Use with "Who Stole the Pumpkin?" on page 43.

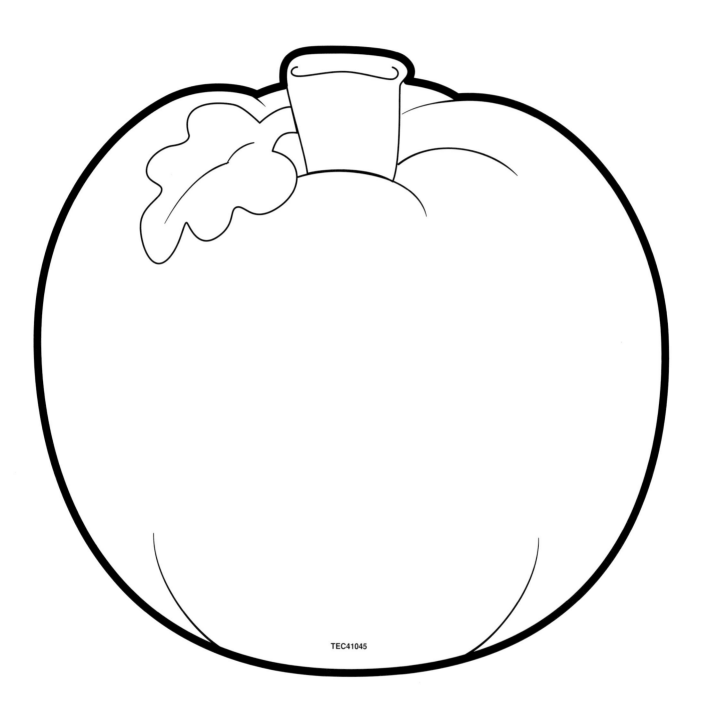

TEC41045

TEC41046

Taste Cards

Use with "Taste-Test Pattern" on page 47.

Salty

TEC41046

Sweet

TEC41046

Sour

TEC41046

Four-Leaf Clover Patterns
Use with "Searching for Clovers" on page 48.

TEC41047

TEC41047

TEC41047

TEC41047

TEC41047

TEC41047

I Spy Letters

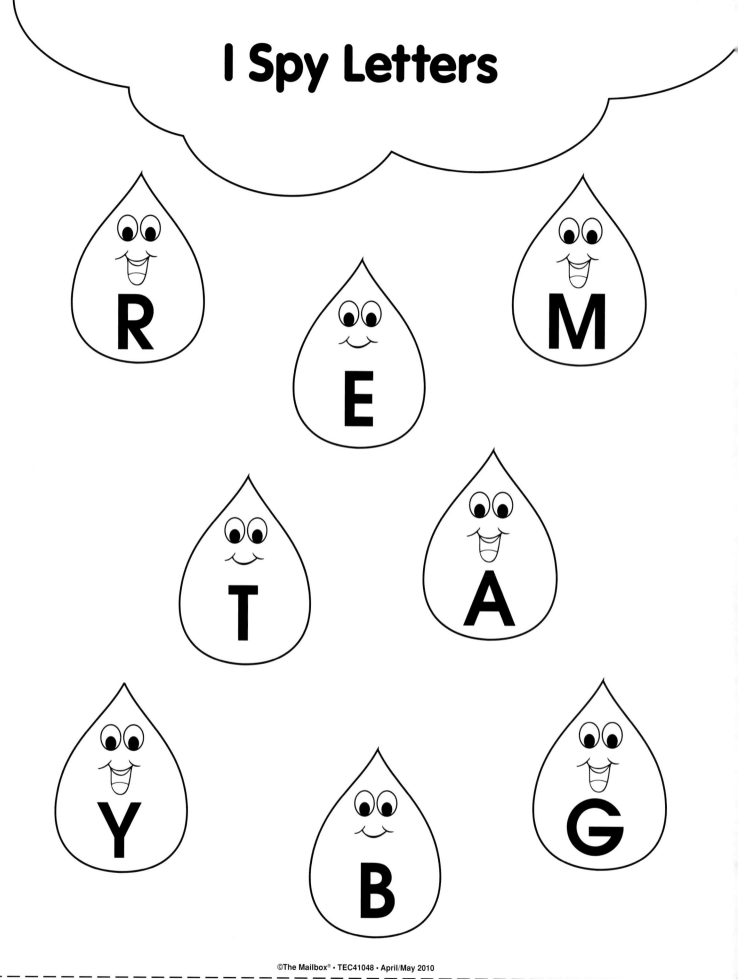

©The Mailbox® • TEC41048 • April/May 2010

62   THE MAILBOX   **Note to the teacher:** Use with "I Spy Letters" on page 53.

CLASSROOM DISPLAYS

CLASSROOM DISPLAYS

Preschool Is Filled With Sunshine!

Have each youngster paint a paper plate yellow and add black hole-punched dots (seeds) to the center of the plate. Trim the plate as shown. Then encourage each child to attach stem and leaf cutouts to the flower. Mount the projects on a board decorated as shown.

Cathy Germino, A Little Folks School House, Manchester, NH

To transform the display for fall, remove a few sunflowers. Add squirrel cutouts (see page 75) and fall leaf crafts. Mount apple crafts on the tree and above a basket cutout near the ground. Title the display "Heading Into Fall!"

For winter, keep the tree and fence but remove all fall-related items. Add red cardinal cutouts (see page 75). Add snowflake crafts to the tree and fence and icicle crafts to the top of the display. Title the display "Winter Is Here!"

For spring, keep the tree and fence but remove all winter-related items. Add butterfly cutouts (see page 75). Add raindrop and spring flower crafts as well as a rainbow. Attach pink tissue paper blossoms to the tree. Title the display "Time for Spring!"

Birthdays Are Special!

Glue rickrack to an oversize poster board cake; then have youngsters decorate the cake using self-adhesive craft foam shapes. Mount the cake on a wall; then attach construction paper candles above the cake. Record each child's name and birthdate on a shape appropriate for his birthday month. Post the shapes around the cake.

Paula Tye-Flagler
McAvinnue Elementary
Lowell, MA

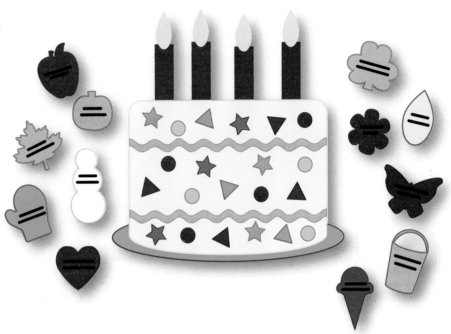

For this adorable display, remove the top flaps from a large cereal box. Then cover it with construction paper and add details so it resembles a crayon box. Help each child wrap construction paper around a cardboard tube and tape the paper in place. Glue a matching paper cone to the top of each tube. Then have each youngster add details, as shown, to make an oversize crayon. Mount the resulting crayon box and crayons on a board with the title shown.

Phyllis Prestridge
West Amory Elementary
Amory, MS

For each child, trace a simple ghost shape on a sheet of paper. Have each child cut out his ghost and then attach a head-shot photo of himself to the ghost. Display the ghosts with speech bubbles and the title shown.

Jaclyn Bussian, YMCA of Dodge County, Beaver Dam, WI

Try this idea for a terrific triangular display! To make a turkey, have each child glue together triangles in different sizes as shown. Then have him use a marker to draw eyes and wings. Attach these shapely projects to a board or wall.

Heather Campbell
Hopewell Country Day School
Pennington, NJ

Harvesting Good Work!

To make this display, attach strips of masking tape to an oversize basket cutout as shown. Have students color the basket with unwrapped brown crayons. Also have youngsters cut from magazines pictures of harvest foods. Attach the basket to a wall and mount the pictures above the basket. Complete the display by posting student work around the basket.

Betty Medlock
Little Blessings Daycare & Preschool
Corinth, MS

Cut out a copy of the house pattern on page 76 for each child and label it with his name and address. Cut the door on the dotted lines; then glue a piece of paper larger than the door to the back of the house, leaving the door unglued. Encourage each child to color the house and draw a self-portrait behind the door. Mount the projects on a board decorated as shown. If desired, use this display to help youngsters recite their addresses.

adapted from an idea by Izetta Thomas
Columbus Reach at Sullivant
Columbus, OH

CLASSROOM DISPLAYS

Have each child transform a black oval into a penguin using a slightly smaller white oval (stomach), a small black circle (head), and construction paper scraps (eyes, beak, feet, and wings). Then encourage him to attach to his penguin a desired accessory, similar to the ones shown. Mount the penguins on a board decorated and titled as shown.

Kim Dessel, Pixie Preschool and Kindergarten, Spotswood, NJ

To make this adorable display, have each child glue a head shot photo to a construction paper rectangle (body). Next, have her attach two construction paper triangles (arms) and a cupcake liner (wings) to the back of the body, as shown. Help her attach a pipe cleaner halo to the resulting angel; then encourage her to use glitter pens to add desired details. Mount the projects on a board with the details and title shown.

Tracey Duvall, Tender Learning Care, Mount Airy, MD

Happy Birthday, Dr. King!

Celebrate Martin Luther King Jr.'s birthday with this display! To make a gift, have each child glue wrapping paper scraps to a construction paper square. Help him trim any overhanging paper; then invite him to attach a gift bow. To complete the gift, attach a tag with the child's description of what he would give to Dr. King. Mount a cake cutout to a wall and post the gifts around the cake; then add the title shown.

Janet Mack, Playful Learning, Laurel, MD

Star Light, Star Bright, Please Don't Let Us Melt Tonight!

For this display, invite each student to decorate a snowpal cutout using assorted collage materials, craft foam shapes, and construction paper scraps. Mount the projects on a board decorated as shown. Then add the title shown to complete the display.

Cindy Farnham, Sheepscot Valley Children's House, Wiscasset, ME

CLASSROOM DISPLAYS

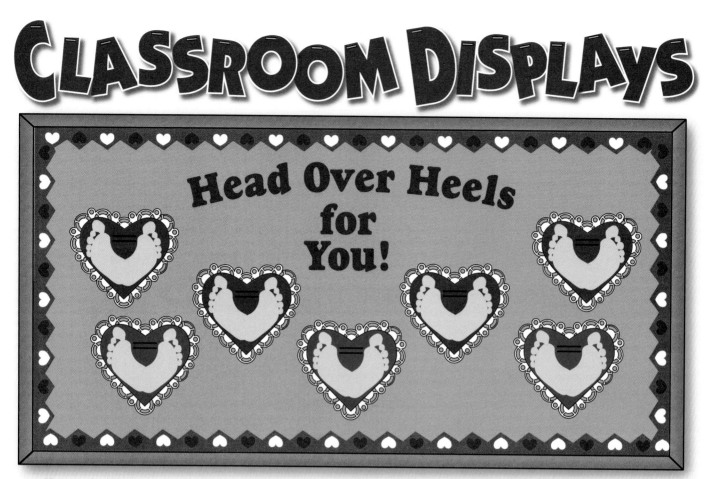

Have each child dip the bottom of one foot in a shallow container of paint and then press it on half of a large heart cutout. Repeat with the other foot, overlapping the prints at the heels. Next, have her glue the heart to a paper doily; then help her write her name and the date on the heart. Mount the projects on a board.

Michele VanBuren, Morrison Day Care, Morrison, IL

What's the Buzz? Spring Is Here!

To make this display, have youngsters apply paint to Bubble Wrap cushioning material and then press it on a large beehive cutout. Also have each child personalize a bee cutout (pattern on page 71). Attach the beehive to a board or wall and mount the bees around the hive.

adapted from an idea by Kim Dessel
Pixie Preschool
Spotswood, NJ

For this adorable display, give each child a blank CD and a photo cutout of himself. Have each child attach his photo to the CD using double-sided tape. Help him use a permanent marker to write his name and the date on the back of the CD. Then use double-sided tape to attach the projects to a wall or door.

Deb Johansmeier
Kids Connection Inc.
St. Charles, IL

Bee Pattern
Use with "What's the Buzz? Spring Is Here!"
on page 70.

TEC41047

CLASSROOM DISPLAYS

You're sure to get a lot of positive feedback about this door display! Have each youngster make a simple duck craft project. Mount the ducks on a door covered with blue bulletin board paper and add details to the display, such as those shown. Then add the title "Waddle On In!" to complete the display.

Tracy Henderson, Brook Hollow Weekday Program, Nashville, TN

For this adorable display, help each child cut slits around the edge of a cupcake liner to make flower petals. Next, have her glue leaf cutouts to a paper stem and then glue the stem to the liner. To personalize the flower, have her glue a head shot photo of herself to the center of the liner. Mount the flowers above a flowerbox cutout with the title shown.

Invite each child to help decorate an oversize umbrella cutout with uppercase and lowercase *R*s. Attach the umbrella to a wall or board. Then give each youngster a raindrop cut from a copy of page 77. Encourage him to name the picture and help him recognize that the name begins with /r/. Have him help attach the raindrop to the display. Then use this rainy-day display to help youngsters practice letter-sound awareness.

Kim Harker, Discovery Express Preschool, Mendon, CT

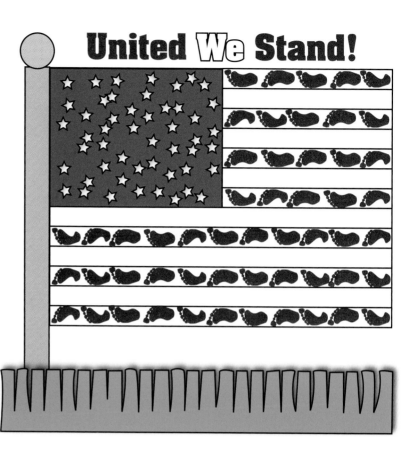

United We Stand!

For this patriotic display, draw a flag outline on a large sheet of white paper. Invite each child to dip the bottom of her feet in a shallow container of red paint; then assist her in walking heel to toe across a portion of an appropriate stripe. Glue a blue paper rectangle to the flag and have youngsters decorate the rectangle with 50 stars. Then mount the flag to a wall.

Heidi McGonegle
Center Point-Urbana Elementary
Center Point, IA

Invite youngsters to make light brown fingerprints on the bottom portion of a length of bulletin board paper so that it resembles a beach. Have each child decorate a person cutout (pattern on page 78) so it resembles himself dressed for the beach. Then attach the beach and the projects to a board or wall and add other cutouts as desired.

Eileen Boughan, Princeton Avenue Preschool, Moorpark, CA

House Pattern

Use with "Home, Sweet Home" on page 67.

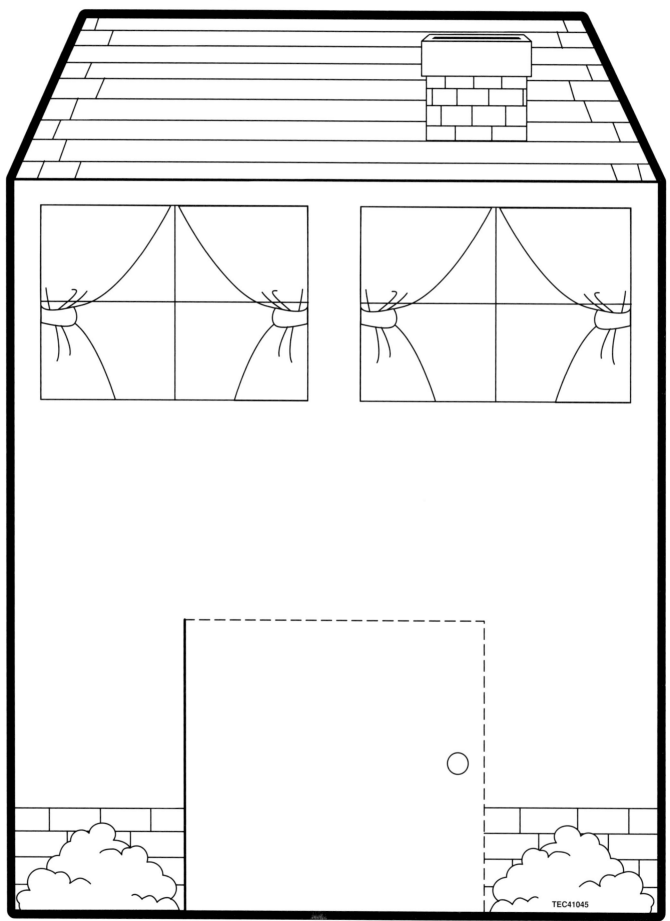

TEC41045

TEC41048

TEC41048

TEC41048

TEC41048

TEC41048

TEC41048

TEC41048

TEC41048

TEC41048

TEC41048

TEC41048

TEC41048

TEC41048

Person Pattern

Use with "Summertime Fun!" on page 74.

TEC41049

KIDS IN THE KITCHEN

KIDS IN THE KITCHEN

Youngsters dip banana slices in two different toppings for this tasty treat!

To prepare for the snack:
- Collect the necessary ingredients and utensils using the lists on the recipe card below.
- Photocopy the step-by-step recipe cards on page 81.
- Color the cards; then cut them out and display them in the snack area.
- Follow the teacher preparation guidelines for the snack.

Double-Dippers

Ingredients for one:
banana half
chocolate syrup
granola

Utensils and supplies:
spoon
plastic knife for each child
plastic fork for each child
disposable plate for each child

Teacher preparation:
Arrange the ingredients and supplies near the step-by-step recipe cards.

Audra Meyerhofer
Long Beach, CA

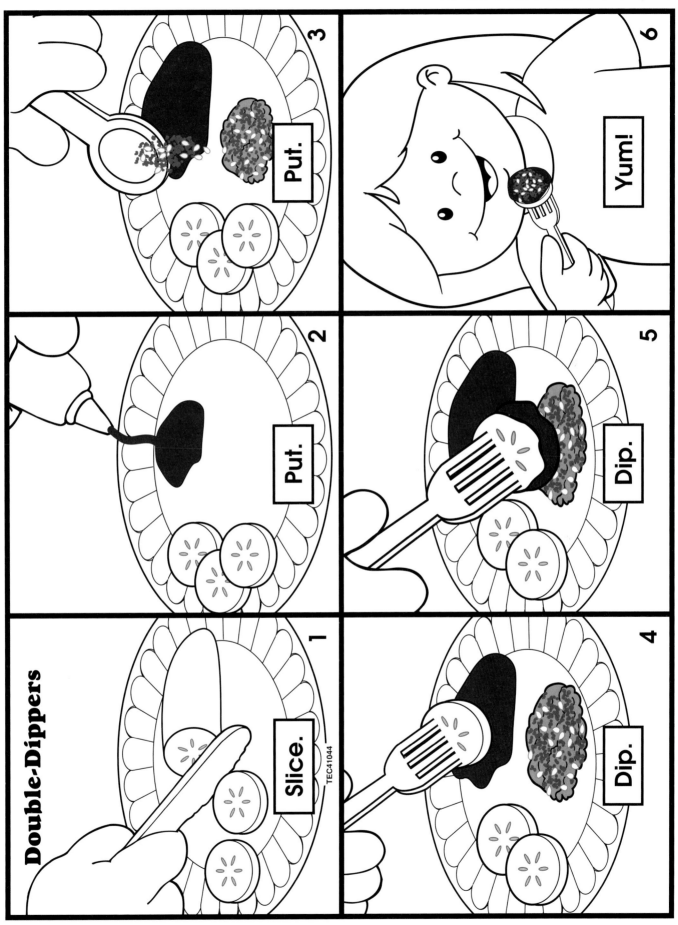

KIDS IN THE KITCHEN

Have youngsters make this spooky yet tasty snack to add to your Halloween celebration.

To prepare for the snack:

- Collect the necessary ingredients and utensils using the lists on the recipe card below.
- Photocopy the step-by-step recipe cards on page 83.
- Color the cards; then cut them out and display them in the snack area.
- Follow the teacher preparation guidelines for the snack.

Spooky House

Ingredients for one:
slice of bread (house)
slice of bologna (moon)
mayonnaise (clouds)
slice of cheese

Utensils and supplies:
disposable plate for each child
plastic knife for each child
pumpkin-shaped cookie cutter

Teacher preparation:
Arrange the ingredients and supplies near the step-by-step recipe cards.

Heather Snider
Oklahoma City, OK

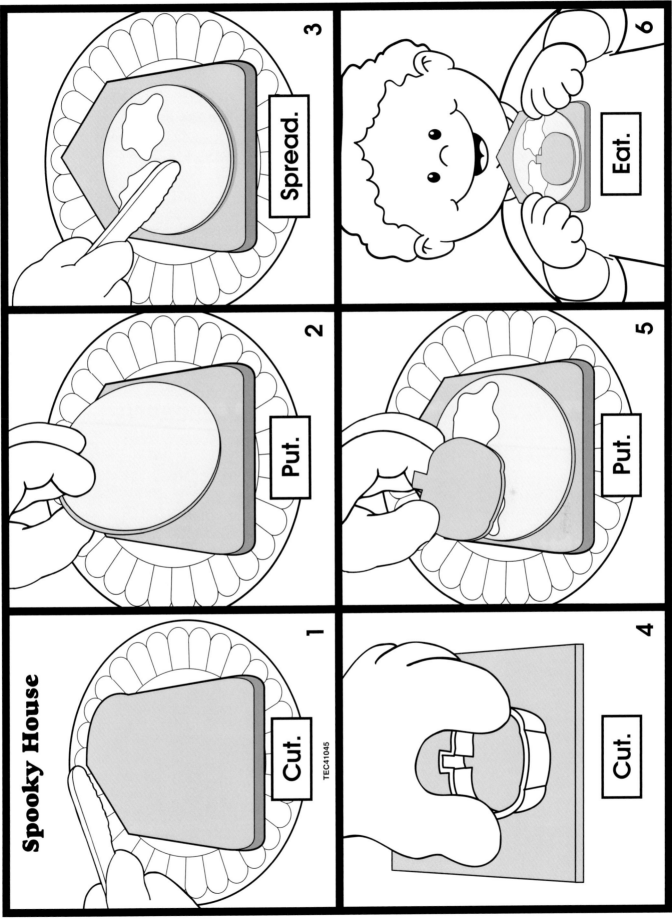

Spooky House

TEC41045

1 Cut.

2 Put.

3 Spread.

4 Cut.

5 Put.

6 Eat.

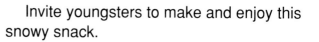

Invite youngsters to make and enjoy this snowy snack.

To prepare for the snack:

- Collect the necessary ingredients and utensils using the lists on the recipe card below.
- Photocopy the step-by-step recipe cards on page 85.
- Color the cards; then cut them out and display them in the snack area.
- Follow the teacher preparation guidelines for the snack.

Winter Tree

Ingredients for one:

pretzel rod half
pretzel sticks
white-frosted O-shaped cereal
white frosting

Utensils and supplies:

paper plate for each child
plastic spoon for each child

Teacher preparation:

Arrange the ingredients and supplies near the step-by-step recipe cards.

Mary Sebastian
Maplewood Preschool
Omaha, NE

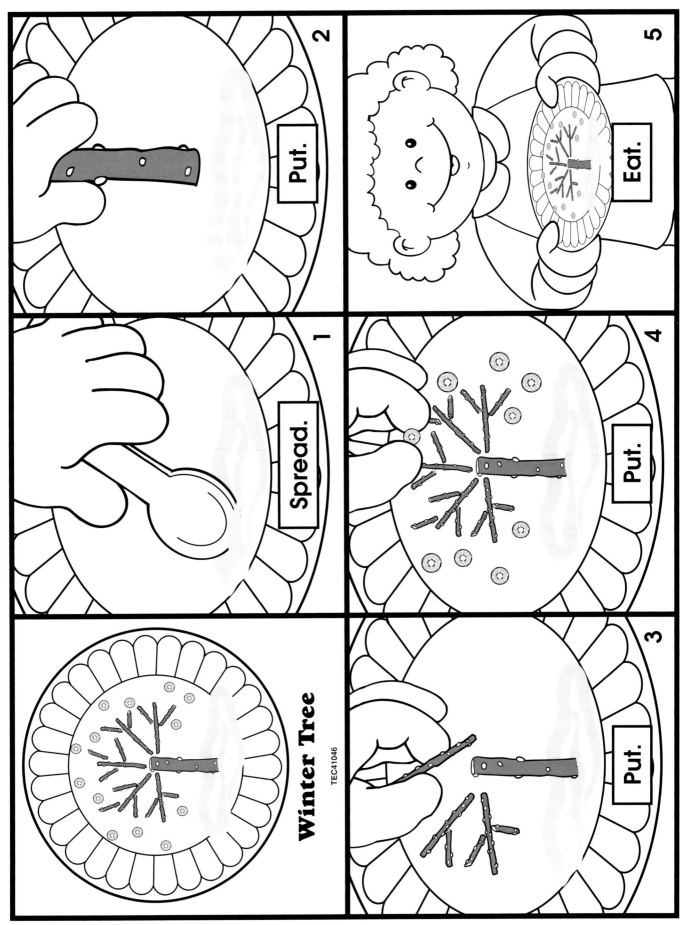

Put. 2

Eat. 5

Spread. 1

Put. 4

Winter Tree

TEC41046

Put. 3

Recipe Cards

Use with "Fishbowls" on page 91.

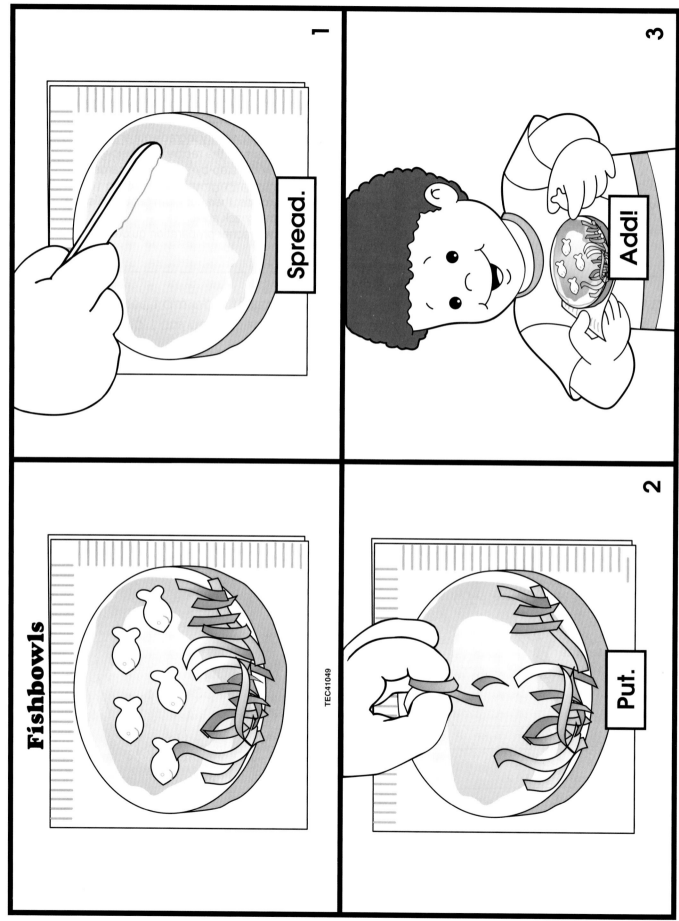

Learning Centers

Hidden Numbers
Math Center

To prepare, mix confetti numbers into a batch of play dough and place the play dough at a center along with cups labeled with corresponding numbers. A youngster uses his hands to manipulate and build with the dough. If desired, he removes numbers from the dough and places them in the appropriate cups.

Michele Sears
Northeast R-IV Cairo/Jacksonville
Cairo, MO

Name Constellations
Literacy Center

Use a white crayon to write each child's name on a separate sheet of black construction paper. Place the papers at a table along with sheets of star stickers. A student visits the center and locates the paper labeled with her name. Then she peels stars from a sheet of stickers and presses them onto each letter.

Phyllis Carollo
Kidsmart, A Learning Childcare Center
Staten Island, NY

Ping-Pong Ball Pickup
Water Table

Float a supply of Ping-Pong balls in your water table. Provide scissor-style salad tongs and a few empty containers. A child manipulates the tongs to grasp a ball; then he removes the ball from the water and releases it into a container. After retrieving several more balls, he spills them back into the water table.

Deborah Yarter
Christ's Church Nursery School
Rye, NY

Shape Connectors
Fine-Motor Area

Cut out several craft foam shapes; then cut a few slits in each shape. Place the shapes at a center. A child lines up two shapes at the slits and then slides them together. He repeats the process, attaching more shapes to his creation.

Kristine Blommel
Stepping Stones
Alexandria, MN

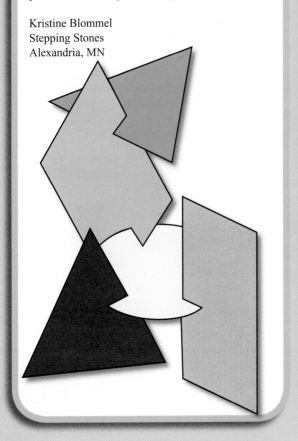

Summer and Fall on the Farm
Sensory Center

Tint rice green and place it in a tub along with farm-related toys. Also provide scoops, cups, and sieves. Have a child visit the center and use the props to engage in pretend play. When fall arrives, remove the green pasture and add yellow rice or rice tinted a variety of fall colors!

Brittany Spriggs, Herscher School District, Kankakee, IL

School Days
Games Center

Obtain stickers and scrapbook paper relating to your classroom theme. Place stickers on the sheet of scrapbook paper between the designs. Then place identical stickers on separate pieces of tagboard to make cards. Laminate the pieces of the game for durability. Then place the paper and cards at a center along with a dry-erase marker. A child chooses a card, finds the matching sticker, and then circles it.

Lynn Francis, Shady Grove UMC Preschool, Glen Allen, VA

Learning Centers

The leaves are turning different colors!

Shayla

Great Eight Spiders
Math Center

A youngster traces a number eight cutout with her finger and says the name of the number. She counts eight black paper strips and glues them to the number to make eight legs. Then she attaches several mini wiggle eyes to the number. What a cute way to learn about the number eight!

Suzy Crawford
Sullivan, IL

GLUE

Nifty Nature
Literacy Center

Gather a collection of natural items, such as autumn leaves, dried grass, pinecones, and twigs. Place the items at a center along with paper and glue. A youngster visits the center and glues items from the collection to a sheet of paper. She dictates information about the items and then contributes her page to a class book titled "Fabulous Fall."

Christina Farley
Seoul Foreign School
Seoul, Korea

Unique Candy Corn
Art Center

Place at a center a supply of construction paper candy corn cutouts along with colorful construction paper scraps, scissors, and glue. A child tears or cuts the paper scraps into small pieces and glues them to a candy corn cutout. Then he trims any paper hanging over the edges of the candy corn, with help as needed.

Tracey Mikos
Sacred Heart School
New Smyrna Beach, FL

Pizza Parlor
Dramatic-Play Area

Put in your dramatic-play area several red felt circles (pizzas). Also provide a variety of felt scraps (toppings) as well as pizza pans, empty seasoning shakers, plastic pizza cutters, aprons, oven mitts, notepads and pencils, a cash register, and play money. A child visits the center and uses the props to engage in pretend pizza parlor play.

Suzanne Foote
East Ithaca Preschool
Ithaca, NY

No Bones About It
Science Center

Obtain two jointed cardboard skeletons from a local party store. Disassemble one skeleton. Place the resulting skeleton puzzle at a center along with the remaining skeleton. A student visits the center and reassembles the skeleton using the duplicate skeleton as a guide.

Marie E. Cecchini
West Dundee, IL

Fancy Pumpkin
Fine-Motor Area

Place several small pumpkins at a table with a variety of craft items, such as self-adhesive foam shapes, yarn, and feathers. A youngster gets a fine-motor workout by attaching a variety of items to the pumpkin to decorate it as desired.

Brenda Moran
Brenda's Little Bizzy Beez
Jacksonville, FL

Learning Centers

Evergreen Explorations
Science Center

Place at a center a collection of small evergreen branches, pine needles, and pinecones. Also provide magnifying glasses, a balance scale, and standard and nonstandard tools for measuring, such as a ruler, a tape measure, ribbon and string. A student uses the tools to investigate the items, comparing the similarities and differences in size, color, weight, scent, and texture.

Marie E. Cecchini

How Many Ornaments?
Math Center

Program each of several die-cut stars with a different number; then attach each star to a separate tree cutout as shown. Provide a supply of colorful pom-poms (ornaments). A child chooses a tree and identifies the number on the star. Then she counts aloud the corresponding number of ornaments and puts them on the tree.

Marie E. Cecchini, West Dundee, IL

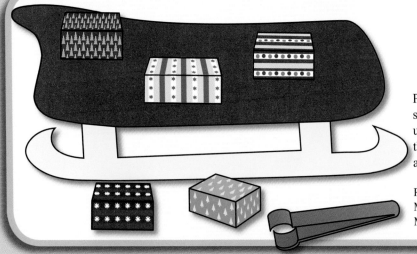

Loading Santa's Sleigh
Fine-Motor Area

In advance, gift-wrap several small boxes. Place the gifts and a pair of tongs near a simple sleigh cutout like the one shown. A youngster uses the tongs to pick up a gift and place it on the sleigh. He continues in the same way until all the gifts are on Santa's sleigh.

Reba Barfield
Marietta First United Methodist Church Preschool
Marietta, GA

Shake, Tip, and Roll
Sensory Center

Fill the bottom of two or three clear plastic bottles with sequins and snowflake confetti. Then fill each bottle with a different liquid, such as water, liquid soap, or vegetable oil. Hot-glue the lid onto each bottle. A youngster manipulates the bottles and observes the similarities and differences in the liquids.

Ana Duplan
South Shore KinderCare Learning Center
League City, TX

Paw Path
Games Center

Make a gameboard similar to the one shown. (Hint: a pawprint stamp is a handy tool for making the path!) Two youngsters each place a bear manipulative on the path. In turn, each student rolls the die and counts aloud the dots on top. Then he moves his bear the corresponding number of pawprints. Play continues in the same manner until each bear reaches the cave.

adapted from an idea by Amy Durrwachter
Kirkwood Early Childhood Center, Kirkwood, MO

Coordinated Snowmen
Literacy Center

Pair snowman and hat cutouts and then label the pairs with matching letters. Place the snowmen and hats in separate piles. A child chooses a snowman. Then she finds the hat with the matching letter and places it on the snowman's head. She continues in the same way until each snowman is wearing the correct hat.

adapted from an idea by Angie Kutzer
Garrett Elementary, Mebane, NC

Learning Centers

Colorful Spool Prints
Art Center

Obtain several plastic thread and ribbon spools in different sizes. Place the spools at a table along with shallow containers of paint and a supply of paper. A youngster dips a spool in paint and then presses it on the paper to make a print. He continues with other spools and colors of paint, overlapping the prints as desired.

Suzanne Foote
East Ithaca Preschool
Ithaca, NY

Clean Sweep
Gross-Motor Area

Use masking tape to make a three-foot square on the floor. Provide a child-size broom along with a dustpan and brush. Scatter items such as cotton balls, pom-poms, or packing peanuts on the floor around the outside of the square. A child uses the broom to sweep the items into the square. Then she uses the brush to sweep the items onto the dustpan.

Janet Boyce
Cokato, MN

Bricks of Gold
Block Center

Wrap several blocks with gold Mylar film or wrapping paper so they resemble gold bricks. Also provide plastic St. Patrick's Day–related hats. A youngster pretends to be a leprechaun and uses the bricks to build a structure made of gold.

Molly Howe
Small Wonders Preschool
Lakeville, MN

Cookie Cereal Letters
Literacy Center

Use a permanent marker to write desired letters on a baking tray. (The marker can be removed using nail polish remover.) Provide a bowl of cookie-style cereal. A student visits the center and places cereal pieces along each letter. When she is finished, she has a small cereal treat from a supply set aside for that purpose.

Kayla Meredith
Kansas City, MO

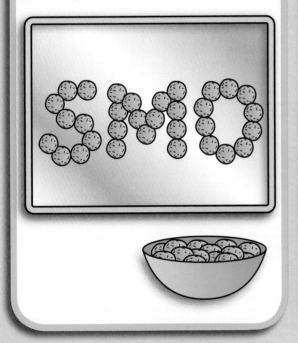

Woolly Lamb

Woolly Lamb
Fine-Motor Area

Place at a table a class supply of page 106 along with green construction paper scraps and a supply of white packing peanuts. A youngster colors the grass in the lamb's mouth. He glues packing peanuts to the lamb so they resemble the lamb's wool. Then he cuts or tears paper scraps and glues them to the bottom of the page to make grass.

Bonnilee Flanagan
Easter Seals Project Excel
Monticello, NY

How Many Cavities?
Math Center

To prepare, place number cards in a pocket chart labeled with the title shown. Draw corresponding numbers of cavities on sets of white construction paper teeth. Place the teeth near the center. A child chooses a set of teeth and counts the number of cavities. Then she places it in the pocket chart next to the corresponding number.

Dana Ann Smith
Donaldsonville Primary School
Donaldsonville, LA

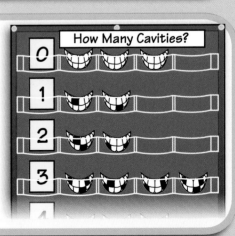

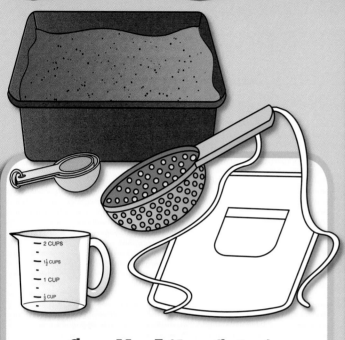

Recyclable Structures
Block Center

Stock your block center with a variety of recyclable items, such as plastic food and drink containers and a collection of cardboard boxes. (Hint: to make less sturdy boxes more durable, stuff them with paper and tape them closed.) A youngster uses the items along with the blocks to create unique sculptures.

Cindy Bryan
Creative Learning Center
Springfield, MO

Smells Like Cake!
Sensory Center

Pour dry cake mix into a large plastic container. Provide items such as an apron, a sifter, measuring cups, and mixing spoons. A child visits the center and uses the props to engage in pretend play. As she plays, she examines the color of the cake mix and sniffs its scent to determine the flavor.

Pam Waldrop
John Wood Elementary
Merrillville, IN

Caterpillar Patterns
Math Center

In advance, use sticky dots to make several different pattern cards like the ones shown. Provide a supply of corresponding-colored die-cut circles for each pattern, programming one circle so it resembles a caterpillar's head. A student chooses a caterpillar pattern card. Then she arranges the circles to copy and extend the pattern.

Leslie Curran
Play Groups
East Setauket, NY

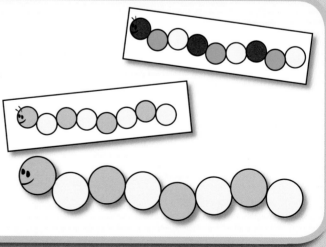

Colorful Kites
Puzzle Center

Draw a kite shape with two intersecting lines, as shown. Provide a supply of colorful triangle cutouts sized to fit the kite's triangle outlines. A student arranges the triangles atop the kite to create his own colorful design. Then he removes the triangles and repeats the activity to create a different design.

Mary Davis
Ankeny Christian Academy
Ankeny, IA

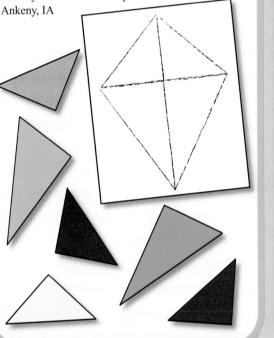

Catching Raindrops
Gross-Motor Area

For this partner activity, attach a raindrop cutout to each of several beanbags and provide a plastic bucket. To play, one child tosses a raindrop in the air and her partner attempts to catch it in the bucket. Play continues in the same way with each remaining raindrop. Then the partners switch places.

Donna Olp
St. Gregory the Great
South Euclid, OH

Shopping Spree
Literacy Center

With this activity, youngsters identify pictures that begin with /k/ as in *cart*. Cut apart the picture cards on page 107. Set out the cards along with a copy of page 108. A student takes a card and says the picture's name. If the name begins with /k/, he puts the card on the cart. If the name begins with a different sound, he sets the card aside. He continues with each remaining card.

Sonya Solomon
Lubavitch on the Palisades Preschool
Tenafly, NJ

Pinch and Clip
Math Center

Provide a supply of spring-style clothespins and several number cards. A student chooses a card and identifies the number. Then he counts aloud the corresponding number of clothespins and clips them to the card.

Betty Silkunas
Lower Gwynedd Elementary
Ambler, PA

Hide-and-Seek Bottles
Science Center

Fill each of two or three clear plastic bottles with a different substance, such as sand, flour, beans, or soil. As you fill each bottle, drop in several small items—such as a rock, a shell, and a button—concealing them in the substance. Hot-glue a lid onto each bottle. A youngster manipulates the bottles to expose the hidden objects.

Keely Peasner
Liberty Ridge Head Start
Bonney, WA

Fantastic Fireworks
Art Center

Set out shallow containers of red, white, and blue paint. Place near each container a bottle brush, pot scrubber, or other handled washer with bristles. A child dips a brush's bristles in paint and then taps, drags, or whisks it on a sheet of black paper. Then she sprinkles glitter on the wet paint.

Bonnie C. Krum
St. Matthew's Early Education Center
Bowie, MD

Tidy Ties
Fine-Motor Center

Recognize Father's Day with this adorable center. Hang a length of clothesline in a traffic-free area of the room. Provide a supply of knotted neckties (or necktie cutouts) along with a container of spring-style clothespins. A student uses the clothespins to attach the ties to the line.

Janet Boyce
Cokato, MN

Which Pail?
Literacy Center

Label fish cutouts with uppercase and lowercase letters, writing one letter on each fish. Then attach a jumbo paper clip to each fish. Scatter the fish on your floor. Provide a small and a large plastic pail along with a magnetic fishing pole. A child uses the fishing pole to "catch" a fish. Then she identifies the letter as uppercase or lowercase. When it is an uppercase letter, she puts the fish in the large pail. When it is a lowercase letter, she puts the fish in the small pail.

adapted from an idea by Susan Pufall
Red Cliff Early Childhood Center
Bayfield, WI

Sweet Scent
Play Dough Center

Scent a batch of red play dough with sugar-free watermelon-flavored gelatin or powdered drink mix. Put the play dough at a table along with a batch of green play dough and a supply of black craft foam seeds. A youngster molds red play dough into the shape of a watermelon slice and uses green play dough to make the rind. Then he tops off the watermelon slice with craft foam seeds.

Heather Leverett
Nashville, TN

Woolly Lamb

Note to the teacher: Use with "Woolly Lamb" on page 101.

TEC41048

TEC41048

TEC41048

TEC41048

TEC41048

TEC41048

TEC41048

TEC41048

TEC41048

TEC41048

TEC41048

TEC41048

Note to the teacher: Use with "Shopping Spree" on page 103.

Management Tips & Timesavers

Management Tips & Timesavers

Revive Your Markers

To extend the life of a dry-erase marker, try this simple tip. Use needle-nose pliers to remove the worn marker tip. Then invert the tip and reinsert it in the marker. Now it works just like new! *DeLynn Martin, Crawford County R-1 School, Bourbon, MO*

Simple Transition

To transition youngsters to a new activity, write an uppercase and lowercase letter pair on the board. Invite a child to choose a letter from the pair and write it on the board. Then send the youngster off to the next activity. *Wendy Hurlimann, Etna Elementary State Preschool, Etna, CA*

Who Is Cleaning?

To motivate little ones to tidy up, sing this song and insert a different youngster's name in each line. Continue singing the song until you've listed all your conscientious cleaners. *Janice Sutherland, Louisiana Schnell Elementary, Placerville, CA*

(*sung to the tune of "Are You Sleeping?"*)

[Child's name] is cleaning.
[Child's name] is cleaning.
So is [child's name].
So is [child's name].
[Child's name] is working so hard.
[Child's name] is working so hard.
So is [child's name].
So is [child's name].

Center Choices

Take pictures of students exploring in various centers and then post the printed photos in the appropriate centers. Encourage youngsters to refer to the photos for appropriate center-time play. *Jessica Miller, Lawson Elementary, Johnston, IA*

Lining Up

Teach youngsters this little trick, and lining up will be quick and easy! Have each child stand at his circle-time seat and face to his right. Your line leader begins walking toward the door. Youngsters follow him, walking around the circle, until everyone is in a straight line waiting to go into the hall. *Jenny Gonsoulin, Saint Edward School, New Iberia, LA*

Management Tips &Timesavers

Busy Boxes

Provide each child with a personalized plastic container. Ask parents to send in items for the container, such as flash cards, puzzles, and coloring books. Invite youngsters to use the materials in their boxes during arrival time, departure time, or free time. *Carol Allen, Harvest Christian Preschool, Griffin, GA*

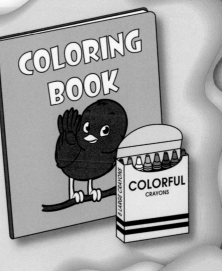

X Marks the Spot

To teach youngsters to use the correct amount of glue, draw a red X wherever glue is needed on a project. Then instruct the child to put a small dot of glue on each X. *Pam Waldrop, John Wood Elementary, Merrillville, IN*

Circle-Time Holder

Stock a large basket with everything needed for the day's circle-time activities. To signal little ones to join you in the circle-time area, grab your basket and sing the following song. *Robin Davila, Crossroads Christian Preschool, Corona, CA*

(sung to the tune of "A Tisket, a Tasket")

A tisket, a tasket,
[Teacher's name] has [her] basket.
It's time for all my little friends
To join me on the carpet.

Your Turn

To indicate when it is a child's turn for a particular task, such as hand washing, sing the catchy tune below and then dismiss the child to complete the task. *Sarah Spaulding, District 206 Early Education Center, Alexandria, MN*

(sung to the tune of "Are You Sleeping?")

Stand up, [child's name]. Stand up, [child's name].
Turn around. Turn around.
Give a little clap, clap,
And a little shake, shake.
[Wash your hands]; then sit down.

Straight Lines

To help youngsters form a straight line without the use of carpet-ruining tape, press the hook side of a length of sew-on Velcro fastener into the carpet. Then have youngsters stand on the Velcro fastener to form their line. *Barb Seeton, Prairie College Elementary, Canton, OH*

Management Tips &Timesavers

Less Mess Painting

When a youngster paints an object such as a disposable cup, have him hold it with a clothespin. This way his hands stay mess free! *Sonia Nieves, Fellowship Methodist Church Parent Day Out Program, Clarksville, TN*

Store and Dispense

Large jugs of glue are economical but not always convenient. Rinse out an empty squeeze bottle such as one used for dish soap. Then fill the bottle with glue from a large jug and store it in a classroom cabinet. Whenever you need glue for a project, simply pull out the bottle rather than dealing with the large jug. *Danielle Rossi, Castle Hill Academy, Medfield, MA*

Candy Cane Kindness

Here's a sweet way to motivate little ones to be kind. Post a large white candy cane cutout divided as shown. Each time a child shows kindness, invite him to color a section of the candy cane. After all the sections have been colored, celebrate with a special treat. *Sue Fleischmann, Catholic East Elementary, Milwaukee, WI*

Time to Share

To help youngsters share a favorite classroom item fairly, use a kitchen timer (sharing bell). Simply set the sharing bell for a designated amount of time. Invite a child to use the item until the sharing bell rings. At the signal, have her pass the item to another youngster. *Sara Sanford, Tiny Treasures, Columbus, OH*

In One Place

For each child, write on a 4" x 6" card important information such as the child's name, address, and medical concerns. Then glue a photo of the child to the back of the card. Place the cards in an inexpensive mini photo album. Since the photo album is compact, it is perfect to take on field trips! *Eileen Gingras, The Children's School at Deerfield Academy, Deerfield, MA*

Management Tips & Timesavers

Lovely Lacing

To help youngsters lace a lacing card correctly, try this tip. Draw lines to connect alternating pairs of holes, as shown. Tell youngsters when they lace the card that the lacing material should cover each line. *Karen Eiben, The Learning House Preschool, LaSalle, IL*

Booklists

On each issue of *The Mailbox*® magazine, write a list of the books featured in that issue. Store the magazines by month. When it's time to plan lessons for the month, you have at your fingertips a list of books that you can use. *Margie Dacheff, Miss Margie's Home Child Care, Spring Grove, IL*

Josh
555-0134

Keeping Records

For each child, gather several index cards. Label each card with a piece of information the child should master during the year. Place the cards in a file box. Use each child's cards to teach and review the information. As a child masters a piece of information, attach a sticker to the card. When it is time to record children's accomplishments, the information is at hand. *Jenny Gonsoulin, Saint Edward School, New Iberia, LA*

Quick Cutting

With this idea, cutting out several patterns at a time is a snap. To keep the sheets of paper from slipping, simply use a binder clip to attach your template to the stack of paper. Then cut around the pattern without worrying about the papers slipping. *Elizabeth Knost, North Kids, Anderson, IN*

Pretty Pages

To keep the pages of student magazines looking good, separate the covers and pages of a magazine. Place each cover or page in a plastic sheet protector. Then simply put the sheet protectors in a three-ring binder. *Erin Hedstrom, Bright Beginnings Childcare, Princeton, MN*

Management Tips & Timesavers

Good Listeners

Use this idea to help youngsters work out small problems for themselves. Each day, invite a child to be the listener. When a student has a small problem, encourage him to share it with the listener. After hearing the problem, the listener helps the youngster determine the best way to solve the problem. *Penny Smith, Ramah Preschool, Huntersville, NC*

Just a Spritz

Here's a less messy way to use watercolor paints. Instead of setting out water cups for youngsters to use, keep a spray bottle of water nearby. When a youngster's tray of paints begins to dry out, simply spritz it with water and let the painting fun continue. *Christina Bailey, H H Browning Primary, Royse City, TX*

Quick Cleanup

Use vinyl placemats to make cleanup quick and easy when using materials such as play dough or shaving cream. Give each youngster a placemat and encourage her to keep the materials on the placemat. When she is finished, simply use a damp cloth to wipe the mat. *Carrie Ryland, Buttons and Bows, Avon, IN*

Sound the Chime

A wind chime is the perfect tool to get youngsters' attention. Hang a wind chime in your classroom. Then sound the chime to signal students to stop and listen. Its soothing sound will make an impression on your little ones! *Erin Hedstrom, Bright Beginnings Childcare, Princeton, MN*

Be Prepared

Prior to naptime, have youngsters place their shoes in a tub. Set the tub by the door. If the group needs to leave the room quickly during naptime, such as for a fire drill, take the tub with you. When students are safely out of the room, have them put their shoes on. *Jackie Bussian, YMCA of Dodge County, Beaver Dam, WI*

OUR READERS WRITE

Our Readers Write

Around the School

On the first day of school I lead my class on a school tour. I take pictures of the staff members we meet and the places we visit. After the photos are developed, I arrange them in a construction paper book and add captions. After sharing the book with the class, I place it in our reading area.

Michele Sears
Northeast R-IV Cairo/Jacksonville
Cairo, MO

This is the playground.

Missing Home

I use my dachshund, Dennis, to help little ones who miss home during the day. I have a toy dog that looks just like Dennis. When a youngster is sad, I tell him I miss my home too because Dennis is there. Then I offer to let him hold the toy Dennis until he is feeling better.

Debra Baldaramos
Rincon Valley Christian Preschool
Santa Rosa, CA

Simple Flannelboard Sets

To make my own flannelboard stories, I print clip art onto T-shirt transfer paper. Then I iron the clip art onto felt pieces and trim the felt as needed. The resulting props are detailed and colorful. Plus they are a fraction of the cost of premade flannelboard sets!

Carole Bogar
Serendipity Preschool
Boardman, OH

Treats for Helpers

My youngsters' parents help me in a variety of ways. To show my appreciation, I attach a sign that says "Thank You" to the front of a box. Then I place inexpensive items—such as candles, notepads, candy, and photo frames—in the box. After a parent has helped in my class, I invite her to choose a treat from the box!

Andrea Henderson
Jefferson Brethren Preschool
Goshen, IN

Thank You

Glitter for Toddlers

I find that this glitter is perfect to use with my young preschoolers. To make a batch of glitter, I mix food coloring and salt; then I spread the mixture out on paper to dry. When the glitter is dry, I store it in a lidded container.

Gayle Brown
Wyckoff Family YMCA
Wyckoff, NJ

Color-Coded

Here's a great way to keep a week's worth of copies organized. To make dividers, I write the name of each school day on a different-colored sheet of paper. Then I stack my copies for the week in order with the corresponding divider atop the copies for that day. This simple idea keeps me organized and is also helpful for substitute teachers in my classroom.

Cindy Kelley, St. Bernard School, Wabash, IN

This and That

Throughout the year, I save leftover materials from our art projects. Near the end of the year, I set out the materials and invite each student to gather desired items in a small paper bag. She glues her items to a piece of poster board to make a collage. Then I display the collages with the title "Everything but the Kitchen Sink."

Dena Stansbury
Grace Children's Learning Center
Manassas, VA

Birthday Crowns

Before parents arrive for open house, I set out a variety of art materials that students will use during the year along with an undecorated crown for each child. Then I encourage parents to experiment with the materials as they decorate a birthday crown for their child. At the end of the evening, I collect each crown and save it until the child's birthday.

Missy Goldenberg
Beth Shalom Preschool
Overland Park, KS

Stir It Up

I found the perfect pointer for little hands. I purchase inexpensive decorative drink stirrers. Then I invite youngsters to use the stirrers to point at charts or big books. My youngsters think these pointers are the best!

Diane Warrenburg
Our Lady of Lourdes
Indianapolis, IN

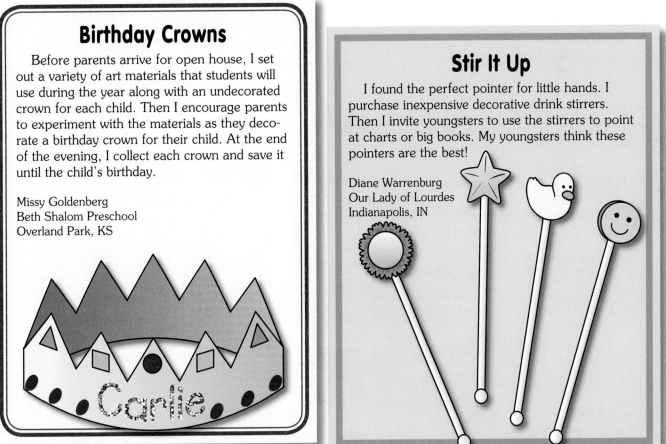

Our Readers Write

Fall Tree

To make this seasonal keepsake, I trace each child's hand and forearm on a sheet of paper to make a tree outline. Then I have him paint the trunk brown and make colorful fingerprint foliage. To finish the keepsake, I have him glue a copy of the poem shown near the tree.

Bobbi Albright
Martinsburg PreK Counts
Martinsburg, PA

My arm and hand have made this tree.
It is a gift to you from me.
So when you see my tree for fall,
Remember me when I was small.

Sammy

You Win

I attach a seasonal cutout to each copy of the newsletter that goes home with my youngsters. But only one cutout has "You win!" written on the back. The family that receives the special cutout sends it back to school with the child. The child then receives a small gift to take home and share with her family.

Mary Campas Valmas
Dasher Green Head Start of Howard County
Columbia, MD

How many Halloween friends do you see? Count with me.

Halloween Counting Book

While my youngsters are wearing their Halloween costumes, I take photos of groups of students with one to five children in each group and one photo of the entire class. Then I print out the photos and attach the class picture to a cover titled "Halloween Counting." I attach each remaining photo to a text page like the one shown. The book quickly becomes a class favorite.

M. Horsley
Valley View United Methodist
Overland Park, KS

One Big Spider

To make this eye-catching spider, we attach a pair of jumbo wiggle eyes to a black latex balloon and black crepe paper legs to a black Mylar balloon. Then we attach the two balloons and legs to the ceiling. I always get many compliments on this supersize class spider!

Linda Remington and Jodi Remington
Busy Day Preschool
Okemos, MI

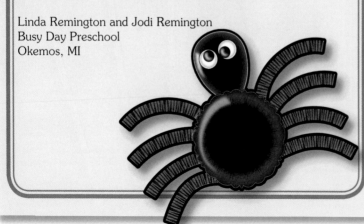

Yummy Pumpkins

For this fun treat, I melt one bag of butterscotch chips in the microwave. Then I mix in one can of white cake frosting and red and yellow food coloring. I allow the mixture to cool. Then I give each child a scoop of the mixture. My students mold the mixture into little balls. Then they push portions of pretzel sticks (stems) into the resulting pumpkins. Finally, they nibble on this special treat.

Cynthia Obrien, Miss Cindy's Daycare, Greentown, PA

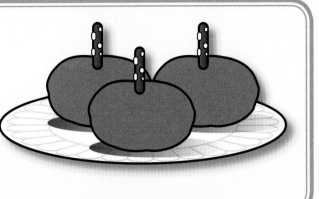

A Silent Snack

I introduced my youngsters to basic sign language that could be used during snacktime, such as the signs for PLEASE, THANK YOU, and MORE. Then I challenge my youngsters to communicate during snacktime using only the signs we learned. They love this silent snacktime and get a fine-motor workout as well!

Lynn Wagoner, Greensboro, NC

A Family Quilt

The director at our center asks each child and staff member to bring in a family photo. Then, in our classes, we glue the photos to a construction paper square. (Each class uses a different color of paper.) We post the squares in a prominent location to create a quilt display. This is a wonderful way to celebrate all of our unique families!

Jennifer Woeller
GV BOCES Child Care Center
Batavia, NY

Magnets and Markers

To create learning opportunities during transition times, I attached a magnetic board near the area where youngsters line up for the restroom. Near the board, I placed colorful magnets and magnetic letters. I use these materials to do quick review activities with my youngsters while they are waiting.

Eve Dutkiewicz
Chavez Learning
Station, Kenosha, WI

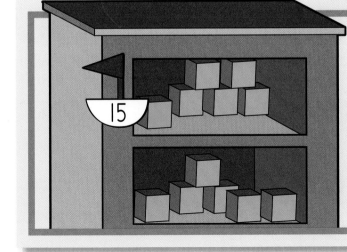

Look and Find

To spice up our calendar time, I hide the calendar cutout for the day somewhere in my classroom. Then I have a child search for the cutout. When she finds it, I encourage her to use positional words to name the location of the cutout. Then I have her attach the cutout to the calendar.

Kristina Wisner
Leaping Learners Child Development Center
Hampstead, MD

Our Readers Write

A Traditional Celebration

To celebrate family traditions during the holiday season, our class has a family luncheon. I ask each family to bring a food item or treat that represents their traditions. For example, one family brought ravioli and gummy fish because they eat pasta and fish for Christmas dinner. A wonderful time was had by all.

Erin McGinness
Great New Beginnings Early Learning Center
Bear, DE

Just Like Rudolph

My classes' favorite holiday story and song is *Rudolph the Red-Nosed Reindeer*. After I read the story and youngsters learn the song, I put a red sticky dot on the end of each child's nose. They love for other students and their parents to see that they have red noses just like Rudolph!

Ann Lipe
Faith Lutheran Preschool
Collierville, TN

Eight Gifts

To teach youngsters about Hanukkah traditions, I put the materials needed for each of eight fun activities in a separate gift bag. Then I display a felt menorah and flames on a flannelboard. Each day of Hanukkah, we "light" the menorah and then open one of the gifts to discover the fun activity for that day.

Marie E. Cecchini
West Dundee, IL

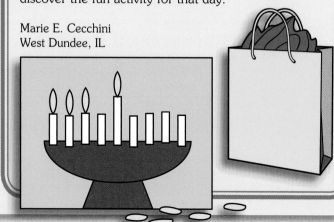

Pumpkin Snowman

What do my youngsters and I do with leftover fall pumpkins? We make snowmen just perfect for winter! I spray-paint three pumpkins white. After the paint dries, we use permanent markers to draw a face and buttons on the snowman. Finally, we add stick arms, a scarf, and a hat. Everyone just loves this fun decoration!

Jessica Stiers
Robert R. Moton Early Childhood Center
Hampton, VA

A Quick Note

I mail out postcards to keep in touch with young-sters in my class over the winter break. On each card I write a note to tell the student how I miss her and can't wait to hear about all the fun things she did during her break. It is amazing how much a quick note means to a child.

Deborah Kohanbash
Hillel Academy
Pittsburgh, PA

Personalized Places

To help my youngsters stay in place during a stage performance, I have each child write his name on a card and decorate it as desired. Then I tape each child's card to the stage where he will stand. During the practice and the performance, I direct each child to stand on his card.

Terri Masters
Reno Christian Church Thursday School
Reno, OH

Munching Monkeys

To encourage little ones to zip their coats, I teach them this trick. I have each child put on his coat and look at the bottom of the zipper. I tell him the opening of the zipper is a monkey's mouth and the other side is a banana. I invite him to practice putting the banana in the monkey's mouth. Then I have him help the monkey eat the banana by pulling up on the zipper pull.

Kimberly Herskowitz
Head Start
Lancaster, PA

Icy Sun Catchers

I have each child put sequins, curling ribbon, and glitter in a disposable pie plate. Then I have her put water in the plate and I place the ends of a yarn hanger in the water. I place the pans outside to freeze. Then I help youngsters pop the frozen sun catchers from the plates and hang them along a fence.

Hayley Hanson
Little Acorns Child Care
Long Lake, MN

Giving to Others

Prior to the holidays, I ask each family to donate a small amount of money and then I plan a field trip to a local superstore. At the store, I enlist students' help in choosing toys for less fortunate children. After we return to school, I invite my little ones to help me wrap the toys.

Katie Greenhaw
Growing Minds Learning Center
Fayetteville, GA

Our Readers Write

Calendar Puzzles

After the beginning of the year, I purchase inexpensive calendars decorated with cute characters. I cut out each large picture and its corresponding small picture from the back of the calendar. I laminate and puzzle-cut the large picture. Then I place the pieces in a resealable plastic bag and tape the matching smaller picture to the outside.

Renee Palumbo
Child's Day Out
Summerville, SC

Stamped With Love

A few days before Valentine's Day, I have each youngster make a card for his family. I help him stamp and address the envelope. Then I take my class on a trip to the post office so each child can mail his valentine. (Contact the post office prior to your visit and the postmaster may allow each child to cancel his own valentine.) My youngsters are so excited when their families receive their valentines in the mail.

Suzy Crawford
Arthur Elementary
Arthur, IL

Valentine Book

I avoid loose valentine cards with this party activity. After each child opens his valentines, I have him glue them to a personalized sheet of construction paper. Then I bind the sheets together to make a supersize book and place the book in my reading area. Youngsters love to look at this Valentine's Day book again and again.

Cathy Patterson
The Learning Center of Westerville
Westerville, OH

Our Sweethearts

Reuse conversation heart boxes to make an adorable display! I take a photo of each child and cut the photo so it fits in the box and can be seen through the window. Then I display the boxes on a board titled "Our Sweethearts!"

Colleen Zeoli
Canna Nursery
Buena Park, CA

Our Readers Write

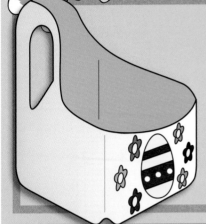

Egg Hunt Jugs

A couple of weeks before our class egg hunt, I send home with each child a milk jug with the top cut off. I also send a note asking parents to help their child create a unique container for egg collecting by decorating the milk jug as desired. On the day of our class egg hunt, each child brings his decorated jug to school. My youngsters and their parents always enjoy this project!

Shelly Post
Helping Hands Preschool
Great Bend, KS

From Egg to Butterfly

To teach youngsters about the life cycle of a butterfly, I ask them to each bring a towel from home. I have each youngster curl up on her towel (leaf) and pretend to be an egg. I encourage her to emerge from her egg as a caterpillar and crawl on the leaf. Next, I have her lie at one end of the towel and roll herself into the towel to form a chrysalis. Finally, I invite her to come out of the chrysalis, place the towel over her shoulders so it resembles wings, and "fly" around the room.

Katie King
Cascade Christian Preschool
Grand Rapids, MI

A Collection of Drawings

I help conserve paper with simple drawing booklets. I staple several sheets of drawing paper between construction paper covers labeled as shown. At our art center, I encourage each child to draw in his booklet. Each youngster can receive a new booklet only when his current one has drawings on the covers and on the back and front of each page.

Selena Grisolia-Merk
West Chester Area YMCA
    Daycare
West Chester, PA

Eli's Drawings

Pretty Piñatas

A newer piñata has a string that opens the door to release the goodies from inside, keeping the piñata intact. I ask parents to donate piñatas that are still in good condition. To introduce a new theme or the letter of the week, I place a related item in a piñata. Then I invite a child to pull the string to open the door and retrieve the item.

Shaunna Johnson
Amazing Kids Preschool
Cameron Park, CA

Working Together

To celebrate Mother's Day, I have each child invite his mother or other special female to a class gathering. During the celebration, I give each pair a wreath cutout and a variety of craft items. As the student and special female work together to decorate the wreath, I take a photo of them. After the photos are printed, I attach each photo to the appropriate wreath.

Iris Burris, Zion Lutheran School, Fallbrook, CA

Bright Backgrounds

Make changing monthly bulletin boards a snap with this tip. Throughout the year, I purchase a length of decorative fabric to correspond with each month. (If desired, buy a few lengths of solid fabrics that can each be used for several months.) I find it is easy to attach the fabric to the bulletin board, plus the fabric can be reused for several years.

Cheryl Ransick, YMCA Preschool, Edwardsville, IL

Tell About It

Assess little ones' use of compound sentences with this tip. I show a child a picture book page that depicts action. Then I ask the child to describe everything that is happening on the page. This is always very effective in helping youngsters generate compound sentences!

Barbara M. Schaeffer, Kiddie Academy, Collegeville, PA

Calendar Match

To make this matching game, I cut pictures from old calendars, including the small pictures on the back of the calendar. I trim each large picture and place it in a sheet protector. Then I glue each small picture to a blank card. To play, a child matches each small picture to the larger picture by placing it in the sheet protector.

Karla Broad
Our Savior Preschool
Naples, FL

A Spring Scene

I celebrate different seasons with this simple drawing activity. As a small group of youngsters looks on, I draw on a sheet of paper something seasonal, such as a flower. Then I give the drawing to a child and encourage her to draw something else that might be seen during the season. We continue in the same way until we have a lovely seasonal picture.

Essra Paddock, Shooting Stars Family Daycare, Warwick, NY

Our Readers Write

Puppet Problem

How does a child use three or more puppets when she only has two hands? With the help of one of my students, I found a solution! I place a few rectangular blocks on the table behind my puppet stage. When a child needs to use more than two puppets, she puts each extra puppet on a block and sets it on the table so it can be seen through the window. Then she is able to complete her show.

Theresa Eumurian
Vineyard Christian Preschool
Anaheim, CA

Not Just for Cookies

Metal cookie sheets work well for activities with magnetic items. However, in my classroom, they have many other uses. My youngsters use them as dry-erase boards, play dough mats, and trays for messy activities, such as writing with shaving cream. Cleanup is a snap! I simply rinse the cookie sheets or wash them in a dishwasher.

Leslie Cedars
Anacoco Elementary
Anacoco, LA

Click It!

I use a simple handheld tally counter to help my youngsters with counting. My youngsters use the counter to count everything from people to shoes to buttons. Sometimes they simply watch the number change as they count! My students love this entertaining and educational gadget.

Janice Sutherland
Louisiana Schnell Elementary
Placerville, CA

Glowing Campfire

Here's a fun way to add that extra touch to your camping unit. We prepare a makeshift campfire by attaching crumpled tissue paper strips to cardboard tubes. Then we turn on a click light and place it under the fire, being sure to completely cover the light with the tissue paper. We turn off the overhead lights and invite youngsters to join us around the campfire to listen to stories and sing songs.

Jodi Remington and Linda Remington
Busy Day Childcare
Okemos, MI

Our Readers Write

Lots of Bubbles

Here's a tip that makes bubble play fun and easy. I pour bubble solution in a dishwashing tub and then give each child a clean flyswatter. She dips the swatter in the solution, removes it, and waves it around. My little ones get so excited when they see all the bubbles they have created!

Karen Decker, Karen's Day Care
Wausau, WI

Take a Memento

Many grandparents who have been unable to visit our classroom during the year come to our end-of-the-year celebration. Prior to the celebration, I prepare a display of photos that have been taken throughout the year. Before the grandparents leave, I invite them to look at the displayed photos and take a few with them. The grandparents love taking these special mementos home.

Kimberly Howells, Chatham Elementary, Pittsburgh, PA

Questions and Answers

In July, I send out a questionnaire to each family with an incoming preschooler. I ask for information about the child's likes, strengths, previous care experiences, and needs. I use this information as an aid in preparing for the first days of school as well as a reference throughout the year. I also ask for a photo of each child, which I use as a cubby tag.

Diane Caughlan, St. John's Lutheran School, Arnold, MO

Seasonal Photo Book

I give parents a year's worth of mementos in this small book. On holidays and other special days throughout the year, I take a photo of each child. (I have the child doing or holding something related to the day.) I help him attach each photo to a piece of coordinating scrapbooking paper. Then I bind all his pages together at the end of the year.

Madelon Corcoran
Miss Madelon's Childcare
Fenton, MI

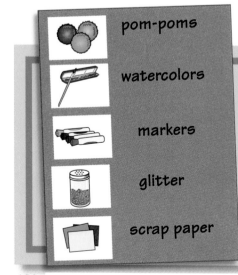

pom-poms

watercolors

markers

glitter

scrap paper

For Your Use

I post a chart so youngsters know what items are available for their use in the art center. To do this, I take pictures of items that are always in the art center, such as pom-poms, watercolors, and stencils. I glue the pictures to a large sheet of construction paper and label them. Then I display the resulting poster.

Lauren Birkhead, New Kent Elementary
New Kent, VA

SCIENCE EXPLORATIONS

Science Explorations

Liquid Layers

With this engaging exploration, youngsters observe and describe liquids that don't mix.

Materials:
clear plastic jar
3 small containers
liquid dish soap
cooking oil
tinted water

STEP 1

Have students observe as you pour a small amount of each liquid into separate containers. Invite each child to touch and smell the liquids and share her observations.

STEP 2

Encourage youngsters to observe as you pour tinted water into the jar. Then say, "I'm going to pour dish soap into the jar as well. What do you think will happen?" Have students share their thoughts. Then pour the dish soap into the jar. Encourage little ones to describe what they see.

STEP 3

Next, tell students that you're going to pour the cooking oil into the jar with the soap and water. Have students predict what will happen. Then slowly pour the cooking oil along the inside of the jar. Youngsters are sure to be excited when three layers form!

What Next?

Place a lid on the jar and secure it with heavy-duty tape. Then place the jar at a center. Encourage youngsters to visit the center and shake the jar. Then have them describe what happens.

Science Explorations

Messy Money

With this exploration, youngsters investigate liquids that will clean tarnished pennies.

Materials:
tarnished pennies
clean penny
container of taco sauce
container of soapy water

STEP 1

Show youngsters the tarnished pennies and the clean penny. Explain that the tarnished pennies once looked exactly like the clean one but that they have gotten dirty. Ask youngsters to share how they might clean the pennies.

STEP 2

Show youngsters the containers of liquids and have them smell and describe each liquid. Name the different liquids. Then have youngsters predict which one will do the best job cleaning the pennies.

STEP 3

Have youngsters help you drop several pennies into each liquid. Encourage them to observe the pennies. Then remove the pennies from the liquids and compare them, prompting students to decide whether their predictions were correct. When the experiment is finished, store the pennies for safekeeping.

What Now?

What other liquids can clean pennies? Have youngsters repeat the experiment with other liquids, such as vinegar, soy sauce, and soda pop.

Science Explorations

Swirling Colors

What happens when you combine dish detergent and food coloring with milk? Your youngsters will be eager to find out with this colorful investigation!

Materials:
dish of whole milk
food coloring
cotton swabs
dish detergent

STEP 1

Show youngsters the dish of milk. Ask students to guess what will happen when you add food coloring to the milk. Then encourage students to help you add drops of food coloring. (Add three or four different colors.)

STEP 2

Encourage a child to touch a cotton swab in the middle of the dish. Prompt little ones to discuss their observations, leading them to notice that the milk and food coloring remain the same.

STEP 3

Have a child dip a cotton swab in dish detergent. Ask youngsters to predict what will happen when they put the detergent-covered swab in the dish of milk. After students share their thoughts, have a child touch the swab to the middle of the dish. Encourage youngsters to watch the milk swirl! Then prompt them to describe their observations.

What Now?

Repeat this investigation with a variety of different liquids. Does any liquid have the same result as the milk?

SONGS & SUCH

SONGS & SUCH

We're So Happy!

Invite students to take their seats for circle time with this sweet little greeting song.

(sung to the tune of "If You're Happy and You Know It")

We're so happy that you're here with us today.
We're so happy that you're here with us today.
We will sing and work and play. We will have a super day!
We're so happy that you're here with us today.

Deborah Keyes
Palm Desert Community Presbyterian Preschool and Academy
Palm Desert, CA

Hand Chant

Here's a quick chant to help students settle in and get ready to listen.

Hands up high.
Hands down low.
Hide those hands—where did they go?
Out comes one.
Out comes two.
Clap them.
Fold them.
Now we're through!

Wiggle hands up high.
Wiggle hands down low.
Place hands behind back.
Reveal one hand.
Reveal the remaining hand.
Clap.
Fold hands together in lap.

Katie Mimmo
Lil' Munchkins
Scituate, MA

The Apple Man

Do your youngsters know who the apple man is? They will after singing this song! Give each child an apple cutout and have him hold it in his lap. Then lead students in singing the song, prompting each child to raise his cutout each time he says the word *apple*.

(sung to the tune of "The Muffin Man")

Oh, do you know the apple man,
The apple man, the apple man?
Oh, do you know the apple man
Who carries apple seeds?

Oh, yes, I know the apple man,
The apple man, the apple man.
Oh, yes, I know the apple man.
He's Johnny Appleseed!

Nancy Madden
Garrison Headstart
Garrison, KY

Magic Soap

Lead students in singing this song as you give them each a drop of hand sanitizer or during their regular hand washing.

(sung to the tune of "Three Blind Mice")

Magic soap, magic soap.
Squirt, squirt here; squirt, squirt there.
It helps to wash all the germs away
So we can eat after we all play.
Oh, don't you love washing hands this way
With magic soap?

Jean Nightingale and Tracy Coan
Denville Community Church Nursery School
Denville, NJ

SONGS & SUCH

Leaves Are Falling

Spotlight colorful fall leaves with this cute little ditty! Lead youngsters in singing the first verse of the song. Then sing the second verse several times, showing students an appropriate leaf cutout before each repetition and changing the color word to match.

(sung to the tune of "The Farmer in the Dell")

The leaves are falling down.
The leaves are falling down.
Heigh-ho! It's fall, I know.
The leaves are falling down.

The leaves are turning [brown].
The leaves are turning [brown].
Heigh-ho! It's fall, I know.
The leaves are turning [brown].

Ginger Cooper, Warren County Head Start, Covington, IN

Pumpkin Faces

Here's a song that helps youngsters demonstrate a variety of emotions.

(sung to the tune of "The Wheels on the Bus")

I like a pumpkin with a [happy] face,
[Happy] face, [happy] face.
I like a pumpkin with a [happy] face
Glowing in the night.

Continue with the following: *scary, frightened, sad, angry.*

LeeAnn Collins
Sunshine House Preschool
Lansing, MI

Time to Eat!

What are some popular Thanksgiving treats? Youngsters have only to sing this song to find out!

(sung to the tune of "Are You Sleeping?")

It's Thanksgiving; it's Thanksgiving.
Time to eat, time to eat!
I like [mashed potatoes]; I like [mashed potatoes].
What a treat, what a treat!

Continue with the following: *tasty turkey, sweet potatoes, pumpkin pie, green beans, apple pie, lots of stuffing.*

Cherie Durbin, Hickory, NC

Fire Safety Song

Lead students in singing this song to teach them about important fire safety rules!

(sung to the tune of "If You're Happy and You Know It")

If you're ever in a fire, don't be scared.
If you're ever in a fire, don't be scared.
There are things that you can do
That will see you safely through.
If you're ever in a fire, don't be scared.

If you're ever in a fire, get out fast.
If you're ever in a fire, get out fast.
Do not stay and don't be slow.
When there's fire, you must go!
If you're ever in a fire, get out fast.

If your clothing is on fire, stop, drop, and roll.
If your clothing is on fire, stop, drop, and roll.
Never run with clothes on fire.
Running makes the flames go higher.
If your clothing is on fire, stop, drop, and roll.

Marcia Jackson, Ashburn Library, Ashburn, VA

SONGS & SUCH

Dreidel Spin

Your little ones are sure to love this simple dreidel rhyme. Encourage them to spin in place as they recite the rhyme and then collapse to the floor during the final line!

Spin like a dreidel,
Round and round.
It begins to slow
And then falls down!

Roxanne LaBell Dearman
Western NC Early Intervention Program for Children Who Are
    Deaf or Hard of Hearing
Charlotte, NC

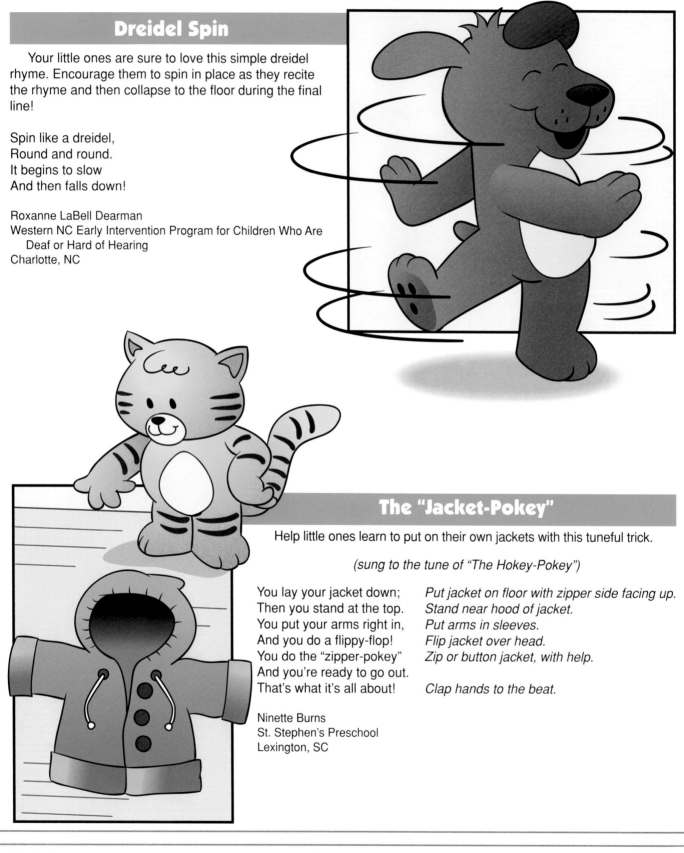

The "Jacket-Pokey"

Help little ones learn to put on their own jackets with this tuneful trick.

(sung to the tune of "The Hokey-Pokey")

You lay your jacket down;   *Put jacket on floor with zipper side facing up.*
Then you stand at the top.   *Stand near hood of jacket.*
You put your arms right in,   *Put arms in sleeves.*
And you do a flippy-flop!   *Flip jacket over head.*
You do the "zipper-pokey"   *Zip or button jacket, with help.*
And you're ready to go out.
That's what it's all about!   *Clap hands to the beat.*

Ninette Burns
St. Stephen's Preschool
Lexington, SC

Happy New Year!

Here's a simple song to help little ones recognize New Year's Day!

(sung to the tune of "This Old Man")

New Year's Day,
It is here.
It's the first day
Of the year.
On this day we celebrate
The year to come.
New Year's Day is
Lots of fun!

Deborah Garmon
Groton, CT

A Little Snowman

Youngsters will be delighted by this sweet song!

(sung to the tune of "I'm a Little Teapot")

I'm a little snowman,
Short and fat.
Here is my scarf.
Here is my hat.
When the sun comes out,
I've got to go!
But I'll be back
The next time it snows.

Hold arms out in front of body to make a tummy.

Touch neck; touch head.

Hold arms up to make a sun.

"Melt" to the floor.

Becky Morgan
Ms Jo's Preschool
Crockett, TX

SONGS & SUCH

A Song for Seuss

Dr. Seuss's birthday is March 2! Celebrate this beloved author with this cute little song. Lead students in singing the song. Then repeat the song five more times, replacing a letter with a clap each time as in the traditional interactive song "Bingo."

(sung to the tune of "Bingo")

There was a man who wrote some books
And Seuss was his name-o!
S-E-U-S-S, S-E-U-S-S, S-E-U-S-S.
And Seuss was his name-o!

Cindy Jewell
Chocowinity Primary School
Chocowinity, NC

I'm a Little Groundhog

Here's a catchy little tune that's just perfect for Groundhog Day!

(sung to the tune of "I'm a Little Teapot")

I'm a little groundhog,
Fat and brown.
I live in my den
Under the ground.
If I see my shadow,
Then I know
We'll have six more
Weeks of snow.

Ellie Brandel
Little Acorns Preschool
Milwaukie, OR

The New Year Dragon

Introduce little ones to the Chinese New Year dragon with this fun song!

(sung to the tune of "The Itsy-Bitsy Spider")

Oh, watch the New Year's dragon.   *Point to eyes.*
He likes to dance around.   *Dance.*
He listens to the music   *Cup hand around ear.*
And makes his growling sound.   *Growl.*
When the dragon dances,   *Dance.*
The New Year can begin,
And we won't see the dragon   *Shake finger to say no.*
'Til a New Year's here again.   *Cover eyes; uncover and look surprised.*

Diana Visser
Castle Academy
Castle Rock, CO

A Valentine Rhyme

Attach to your board five heart cutouts in the colors shown. Lead students in singing the song and then removing the pink heart. Continue with the suggestions given, removing each remaining heart when appropriate.

(sung to the tune of "Five Little Ducks")

Five little valentines I once knew—
All lined up for us to view.
But the valentine that rhymes with [*ink*],
That is my favorite! It's the color [pink],
Color [pink], color [pink].
That is my favorite! It's the color [pink].

Continue with the following: *bed, red; shoe, blue; light, white; bean, green.*

Cari Charron, Child Care Resource and Referral, Quesnel, British Columbia, Canada

SONGS & SUCH

Colorful Easter Eggs

Youngsters recognize colors with this adorable Easter chant! Give each child a colorful egg cutout. Then lead students in reciting the chant, prompting youngsters with yellow eggs to move as indicated. Repeat the rhyme several times, substituting a different color each time.

It's Easter time; it's Easter time.
That means it's time to do the bunny rhyme!
All the bunnies with [yellow] eggs,
Hop with your furry bunny legs.
Hop up high and hop down low.
Hop really fast; then hop really slow.

Wonderful Spring!

Here's a springtime song that youngsters are sure to enjoy!

(sung to the tune of "If You're Happy and You Know It")

Well, it's springtime, and I'm oh so very glad! (It's here!)
It's not winter anymore, but I'm not sad! (It's here!)
Rain falls down and flowers bloom
And there's no more winter gloom.
Well, it's springtime, and I'm oh so very glad! (It's here!)

Five Little Tadpoles

Hop to it and teach your preschoolers this poem about tadpoles that will soon become frogs. Ribbit!

Five little tadpoles swimming near the shore.
The first one said, "Let's swim some more!"
The second one said, "Let's rest awhile."
The third one said, "Swimming makes me smile!"
The fourth one said, "My legs are growing long!"
The fifth one said, "I'm getting very strong!"
Five little tadpoles will soon be frogs.
They'll jump from the water and sit on logs.

Lenny D. Grozier
Binghamton, NY

It's a Rainbow!

Little ones learn the colors of the rainbow with this simple song!

*(sung to the tune of
"Twinkle, Twinkle, Little Star")*

Red, orange, yellow, green and blue,
Indigo, and violet too.
Rainbow, rainbow in the sky.
Rainbow, rainbow way up high.
Red, orange, yellow, green and blue,
Indigo, and violet too.

Marie E. Cecchini, West Dundee, IL

SONGS & SUCH

Splendid Summertime!

Usher in this fantastic season with a super song selection!

(sung to the tune of "Yankee Doodle")

Summertime is lots of fun.
There is so much to do—
Swim in lakes and sail on boats
And play on beaches too.
Summertime is so much fun.
We're so glad it's here.
Don't you think that summer is
The best time of the year?

Deborah Garmon
Groton, CT

A Trip to the Zoo!

What will youngsters see at the zoo? Highlight a few popular zoo sights with this chant! Encourage youngsters to make up actions to go with each line of the chant.

We're taking a trip to the zoo.
We may see a monkey and kangaroo!
We're taking a trip to the zoo
Where big giraffes look down on you!
We're taking a trip to the zoo
Where mighty owls go, "Whoo, whoo, whoo!"
We're taking a trip to the zoo,
And we'll do the dance that the ostriches do!

Cyndi Smith
Louisville Childcare Center
Louisville, OH

Construction Time

Have little ones make up motions to match each verse of this catchy little ditty!

(sung to the tune of "The Wheels on the Bus")

The excavator scoops up all the dirt,
All the dirt, all the dirt.
The excavator scoops up all the dirt
At the construction site.

Continue with the following:
The dump truck takes the dirt away.
The bulldozer flattens out the ground.
The crane picks up the heavy steel.

Linda Nance
Calvary Baptist Preschool & Kindergarten
Anaheim, CA

A Summer Fruit Song

If desired, have youngsters make a tasty fruit salad after you lead them in singing this entertaining song!

(sung to the tune of "Are You Sleeping?")

Watermelon, watermelon.
Strawberries, strawberries.
Honeydew and peaches, honeydew and peaches.
Cantaloupe, cantaloupe.

Emeline Holmes
Lighthouse Kiddie Kampus & Day Care
Fond Du Lac, WI

Ocean Waves

This action rhyme is almost as much fun as an actual trip to the beach!

I went to the ocean	*Point to self.*
To see the waves there.	*Move arms to resemble waves.*
The wind blew gently	*Wiggle fingers.*
And ruffled my hair.	*Move fingers through hair.*
I scooped up some sand	*Pretend to scoop sand.*
And packed it really tight.	*Squeeze the pretend sand.*
Then I made a sand castle.	*Pat floor as if patting sand.*
What a beautiful sight!	*Throw out arms.*

Deborah Garmon
Groton, CT

Five Little Balloons

Your youngsters will love this silly chant about five little balloons in a store. If desired, attach five balloon cutouts to a wall and have students remove a cutout after each verse. For added fun, prompt students to clap loudly each time they say, "Pop!"

Five little balloons bobbing in a store—
One went "Pop!" and then there were four.
Four little balloons—each one is free;
One went "Pop!" and then there were three.
Three little balloons so shiny and new—
One went "Pop!" and then there were two.
Two little balloons—balloons are fun!
One went "Pop!" and then there was one.
One little balloon got caught in the door.
It went "Pop!" and there were no more!

Shelley Hoster
Jack & Jill Early Learning Center
Norcross, GA

Storytime

Little Blue and Little Yellow
Written and illustrated by Leo Lionni

little blue and little yellow
by Leo Lionni

Little Blue and Little Yellow are best friends who love to run and play together! One day they are so overjoyed to see each other that they hug and hug until they turn green! How will anyone recognize them?

ideas contributed by Ada Goren, Winston-Salem, NC

Before You Read

Tell youngsters that today's story is about two best friends named Little Blue and Little Yellow. Then display a resealable plastic bag containing a blob of blue fingerpaint in one corner and a blob of yellow fingerpaint in the opposite corner. Ask youngsters to predict what they think will happen if the two blobs hug. After each child has had a chance to respond, read aloud this classic story. Then manipulate the bag and have youngsters observe the colors combining to form green!

Marcus

Little Blue and Li...

Angel

Little Red and Little Yellow

After You Read

Invite youngsters to paint a portrait of Little Blue and Little Yellow, of Little Red and Little Yellow, or of Little Blue and Little Red. Place at a table separate containers of paint along with a supply of paper programmed with two intersecting circles, as shown. Encourage youngsters to paint each circle with a different color of paint, overlapping the paints in the center to create a new color. Label each painting appropriately.

If You Give a Mouse a Cookie

Written by Laura Joffe Numeroff
Illustrated by Felicia Bond

When a young boy gives a mouse a cookie, the mouse wants a glass of milk. As the consequences of this simple action build, the boy gets more and more tired, yet the mouse is filled with energy!

Before You Read

Conceal several items from the story in a bag. You might consider using a toy mouse, a cookie, a small milk container, rubber gloves, a sponge, and crayons. Have students help you remove and identify the items. Tell students that the items appear in the story you're about to read. Invite little ones to share what they think happens in the story. Then read this engaging tale aloud and compare it to little ones' imaginative version.

adapted from an idea by Sanita Arora; Rainbow United, Inc.; Wichita, KS

After You Read

Invite youngsters to make this adorable mouse puppet, which is sure to inspire a retelling of this delightful story! Have each child decorate a construction paper mouse cutout similar to the one shown. Then have him attach a jumbo craft stick to the back. Next, encourage him to describe how to make his favorite cookie. Record his recipe idea on a small card. Finally, have him attach the recipe card and a decorated cookie cutout to the mouse, as shown. Now that's one yummy cookie recipe!

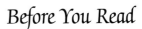

Chocolate-Chip Raisin Cookie

adapted from an idea by Sarah Booth, Messiah Nursery School, Williamsport, PA

Storytime

Go Away, Big Green Monster!
By Ed Emberley

Yellow eyes, purple hair, and sharp white teeth sure sound scary! But not to worry! Thanks to clever cutout pages, this big green monster leaves just as quickly as it appears.

ideas contributed by Lucia Kemp Henry, Fallon, NV

> I would act like a dinosaur and stomp my feet and roar!

Before You Read

Display the cover of the book and read the title aloud. Then ask little ones whether they think monsters are real or pretend. Encourage youngsters to explain their thoughts; then lead them to understand that monsters are pretend. Next, inspire students' creative thinking by inviting them to tell how they would make an imaginary monster disappear. Finally, read the book aloud to reveal how the author makes the big green monster disappear!

You don't scare Kevin,

so go away!

And don't come back

until KEVIN says so!

After You Read

Invite each child to create a monster he can make disappear! For each child, fold a 12" x 18" sheet of construction paper to make two equal flaps that meet in the middle of the paper. Program the outside and interior as shown. Encourage each child to draw a colorful monster in the middle of the paper. Then invite him to reveal his monster as you lead the group in chanting the sentence on the inside. Finally, have the child close the flaps as the group chants the remaining words.

Mouse Mess

Written and illustrated by Linnea Riley

Just as the family heads upstairs to bed, a tiny mouse wakes up with an enormous appetite! This mischievous midnight muncher merrily eats his way through every morsel of food in the kitchen, leaving the place a huge mess!

> The mouse eats too much and gets a tummy ache!

Before You Read

Display the back of the book and ask students to name different foods they see. Next, show the front of the book, pointing out the tiny critter balancing on the stack of crème-filled cookies. Then ask little ones to predict what they think happens to the mouse in the story. After youngsters share their thoughts, read aloud this rollicking tale of a mouse's midnight munching and have little ones see whether their predictions came true.

After You Read

Give each child a sheet of paper programmed with the prompt shown. Ask her to pretend she is a little mouse who wakes up hungry for a midnight snack. Read the prompt aloud and encourage her to name something she would eat. Record her dictation; then have her illustrate the page. If desired, bind the pages together to make a class book titled "Midnight Munchers."

If I were a mouse, I would eat <u>cookies, pizza, and a hot dog</u> for a midnight snack!

by <u>Kayla</u>

Storytime

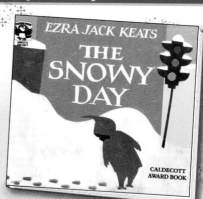

The Snowy Day
Written and illustrated by Ezra Jack Keats

Peter wakes up one morning to discover that snow has fallen overnight. He makes tracks in the snow and makes a snowman and snow angels. This classic story and its simple illustrations will charm your youngsters.

ideas contributed by Ada Goren, Winston-Salem, NC

> I would like to throw snowballs at my brother!

Before You Read
Gather an oversize wad of cotton batting and tell students they are going to pretend it's snow. Give the snow to a child and have her share what she would like to do on a snowy day. After each student has the opportunity to share her thoughts, tell youngsters that the story you're about to read has a little boy who enjoys several snowy day activities.

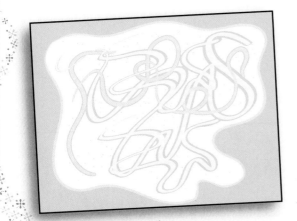

After You Read
To make textured paint (snow), mix white tempera paint and flour. Revisit the page spread that shows the tracks Peter makes by dragging a stick in the snow. Then help each child spread a thick layer of snow on a sheet of tagboard. Have her use a stick to draw lines in the snow just as Peter does!

Merry Christmas, Big Hungry Bear!

Written by Don and Audrey Wood
Illustrated by Don Wood

When little Mouse is reminded of the big, hungry Bear at the top of the hill, he takes steps to protect his Christmas presents. But when he learns that Bear never gets any presents, he has a sudden change of heart!

> Mouse is happy because it's Christmas!

Before You Read

Display the cover of the book and ask little ones to describe how they think Mouse is feeling. Then ask, "Do you think the presents under the tree are for Mouse, or is Mouse going to give the presents to someone else?" After each youngster has a chance to share his thoughts, encourage him to tell how he feels when he receives a gift and when he gives a gift to someone else. Finally, have youngsters settle in for this entertaining read-aloud that highlights the importance of generosity and sharing.

After You Read

Give each child a sheet of paper programmed with the prompt shown. Then show youngsters a picture of the gift box that the bear gives the mouse. Read the prompt aloud and encourage each youngster to draw a picture of what she thinks is in the box; then have her dictate a response to complete the prompt. Finally, help her staple a gift wrap cover over her work. Then invite her to attach a gift bow to the cover.

For Christmas, Bear gives Mouse...
a giant piece of cheese and a big box of crackers!

Alexa

Storytime

Llama Llama Red Pajama
Written and Illustrated by Anna Dewdney

After kissing Baby Llama good-night, Mama makes her way downstairs. Then, as Mama Llama does some chores, Baby Llama begins some bedtime drama!

ideas contributed by Lucia Kemp Henry, Fallon, NV

Before You Read

Display the cover of the book and have students describe what they see in the setting. Ask little ones to study the llama's expression, describe how he is feeling, and consider why he might feel that way. Then have students predict what they think happens in the story. After youngsters share their thoughts, have them settle in for this entertaining read-aloud to see whether their predictions come true.

I think he's afraid of the dark!

After You Read

Use a pillow and a blanket to make a pretend bed on your floor. Gather youngsters around the bed. Then ask each child to name something she does to settle down for bedtime. Write each youngster's words on a separate index card and have her place her card on the bed.

Tuesday

Written and Illustrated by David Wiesner

One Tuesday evening, a curious event takes place. A fleet of frogs fly atop lily pads through an unsuspecting town. The illustrations in this nearly wordless picture book will tickle both your youngsters and you.

A frog would hop!

Before You Read

Before revealing the cover of the book, invite little ones to name things a frog might do. Write youngsters' responses on a large lily pad cutout. Tell students that the book you're about to share shows frogs doing something very unusual. Finally, read this fantastic frog tale aloud!

After You Read

Have each child attach a moon cutout to a sheet of construction paper labeled with the prompt "One Tuesday." Encourage him to dictate words to describe something odd that happens one Tuesday. Then have him illustrate his words. If desired, display the work on a board with foil stars and the title "One Tuesday…"

One Tuesday, a rabbit roller-skates and eats a carrot!
William

Storytime

Pancakes, Pancakes!
Written and illustrated by Eric Carle

Jack wakes up one morning with one thought on his mind—having a big pancake for breakfast! So he sets out to gather all the necessary ingredients, discovering that it takes quite a bit of work to make a pancake!

> I think Jack wants pancakes for breakfast!

Before You Read
Conceal in a bag a container of flour, a plastic egg, a milk container, and a margarine tub. Tell little ones that today's story is about a boy named Jack who asks his mother to make something special for breakfast. Then have youngsters help you remove and identify the items. Tell students the items are used to make the food Jack wants. Then ask them to predict what they think Jack asked his mother to make. Finally, display the cover of the book and read aloud its title so students can see whether their predictions were correct. Then read the story aloud.

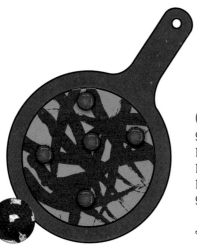

After You Read
Set out a frying pan, brown circle cutouts sized to fit the pan (pancakes), a squeeze bottle filled with red paint (strawberry jam), a golf ball, and a supply of red pom-poms (strawberries). Have a child put a pancake in the frying pan. Then help him squeeze jam on the pancake. Next, encourage him to roll the golf ball around on the pancake. Have him press strawberries in the jam. Finally, help him glue his pancake to a frying pan cutout.

Jessica McEwen, Great Beginnings Learning School, Danvers, MA

Planting a Rainbow

Written and illustrated by Lois Ehlert

A mother and child delight in their tradition of planting flower bulbs, seeds, and plant seedlings and then watching them grow into a rainbow of colorful blooms.

A rainbow doesn't grow! It's in the sky!

Before You Read

Before revealing the cover of the book, ask youngsters if they have ever seen a rainbow. Encourage students to tell about the rainbow and the colors they observed. Then ask little ones if anyone has ever grown a rainbow. No doubt youngsters will tell you such a thing isn't possible. Next, display the cover of the book and read its title aloud. Then have little ones settle in for this colorful read-aloud that reveals how a mother and child grow a beautiful rainbow.

After You Read

Have each child paint the bottom of a sheet of construction paper brown. Then have her paint six green stems with leaves. Next, review the sequence of rainbow-colored flowers near the end of the book. Then encourage her to use craft foam shapes to make her own unique rainbow of flowers.

Storytime

Blueberries for Sal

Written and illustrated by Robert McCloskey

Little Sal and her mother go to Blueberry Hill to pick blueberries. Little Bear and his mother go to Blueberry Hill to eat blueberries. When Little Sal and Little Bear wander off and then trail after the wrong mothers, there are hilarious results!

ideas contributed by Ada Goren, Winston-Salem, NC

Before You Read

Scatter a class supply of play dough blueberries on a bush cutout and set a pail nearby. Tell students they are going to pretend they are picking blueberries. Have the group listen carefully as three classmates at a time each "pick" a berry and drop it in the pail. Then ask youngsters to mimic the sounds the berries made when they were dropped. Finally, introduce the book and tell students to listen for the sounds the berries make when Sal drops them in her pail.

Kuplink, kuplank, kuplunk!

After You Read

Cut out two copies of the cards on page 160 and place them facedown on the floor. To play this version of Concentration, invite youngsters, in turn, to flip two cards. When a match is found, set the cards aside. If a youngster reveals two blueberry cards, encourage her to say, "Kuplink, kuplank, kuplunk!" to match the sounds in the story. Then have her set the cards aside. The game is finished when all the cards are matched!

The Giant Jam Sandwich
Written and illustrated by John Vernon Lord
With verses by Janet Burroway

One summer day, a gigantic swarm of wasps invades the town of Itching Down. So the townspeople devise an ingenious plan to rid themselves of this horrific nuisance!

The wasp gets in somebody's house and stings him!

Before You Read
Display the cover of the book and ask youngsters to name how many critters they see. After determining that there is just one wasp, ask little ones to predict what they think happens in the story. After students share their thoughts, have them settle in for this surprising tale to see whether their predictions are correct.

After You Read
Give each child two large construction paper bread slices, with one slice programmed as shown. Have each child fingerpaint the blank slice with red paint (strawberry jam). Read the prompt aloud and encourage each student to draw on a separate paper something he might catch in his sandwich. Then have him cut out the picture and attach it to the jam. Finally, record his description of what he caught; then help him staple the sandwich along the left side.

In my giant jam sandwich, I caught...

three big spiders!

Picture Cards
Use with "After You Read" on page 158.

TEC41049

TEC41049

TEC41049

TEC41049

TEC41049

TEC41049

TEC41049

TEC41049

TEC41049

TEC41049

TEC41049

TEC41049

BOOK UNITS

Kitten's First Full Moon

By Kevin Henkes

When Kitten sees a full moon for the first time, she's sure it's a big bowl of milk just waiting to be lapped up! Kitten's attempts to reach the moon are unsuccessful and she ends up tired, wet, and sad. Fortunately, there is a surprise waiting for her at home. Lucky Kitten!

ideas contributed by Ada Goren, Winston-Salem, NC

Is It the Moon?
Developing interest in the story

Before reading the story, attach a white paper plate, a cotton ball, and an inflated white balloon to a wall. To begin, turn out the lights. Then turn on a flashlight and shine it on the paper plate. Say, "Oh my goodness—it's the moon!" Youngsters will no doubt scoff and inform you that it's just a paper plate. Explain that you thought it was the moon because it is white and round. Repeat the process with the balloon and the cotton ball. Then present the book, explaining that the kitten in the story gets confused as well, thinking that the moon is really a bowl of milk! Have students settle in for this award-winning read-aloud.

Black and White
Responding to a story through art

Revisit the illustrations in the book and guide youngsters to notice that all the illustrations are black and white. To have each student make his own black-and-white illustration, encourage him to use a white crayon to draw a scene from the book on white paper. Then invite him to brush black watercolor paint over the entire surface of the paper.

Poor Kitten!
Participating in a story
To make a prop to use during a rereading of the story, give each child two kitten head cutouts. Invite her to draw a happy face on one cutout and a sad face on the remaining cutout. Help her glue a jumbo craft stick between the faces. During a read-aloud, encourage youngsters to hold up the sad kitten faces and chant, "Poor Kitten!" when appropriate. At the end of the story, encourage youngsters to hold up the happy kitten faces and chant, "Lucky Kitten!"

Kitten almost ate a bug.

Kitten got some milk.

The kitten fell in the pond.

My Favorite Part
Writing
Cover a board with black paper. Then add a moon cutout and a kitten cutout to the display. Invite each child to share his favorite part of the story as you write his words on a star cutout. Have him brush glue over portions of the star and then place the star in a small tub of glitter. Encourage him to sprinkle glitter over the glue and tap off the excess. Post the stars on the display.

Mouth.

Milk and Moon
Identifying beginning sound /m/
Youngsters listen for /m/ with this activity, which extends the themes found in the story. Have students say the word *moon* and have them listen carefully for the /m/ sound. Encourage them to repeat the process with the word *milk*. Then give each child a white paper plate (moon). Say several different words, encouraging students to raise their moons in the air if the word begins with /m/ and keep their moons lowered if the word does not.

Five Days With a Familiar Story:
Rosie's Walk

Written and illustrated by Pat Hutchins

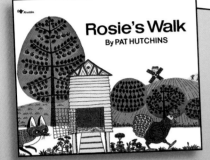

A hen named Rosie goes for a walk around the farmyard and is followed by a sneaky and accident-prone fox. With this fun unit, you can do a different activity each day of the week or pick and choose your favorites! What a fun way to present this classic story to your little ones!

ideas contributed by Roxanne Labell Dearman
Western NC Early Intervention Program for Children Who Are Deaf or Hard of Hearing
Charlotte, NC

Day 1

Let's Go Walking
Building anticipation for the read-aloud

Before reading the story, gather youngsters for a walk around your room or school. As you lead them, narrate your path using positional words. For example, you might say, "We are walking over the carpet, beside the table, and next to the reading center." Every few moments, stop the game and ask students whether anyone is following them. When students conclude that they have no followers, continue the game. Then have little ones sit in your storytime area. Explain that the story you're about to read is about a hen who takes a walk just like they did, but there is a creature following her every move! Then have students settle in for the read-aloud.

Splash!

Rosie the hen went for a walk

across the yard

around the pond

over the haystack

Day 2

Sound Effects
Recalling story details

Write the text from the story on sentence strips and place the strips in a pocket chart. Reread the story to your youngsters. Then read aloud the strips as you point to the words, pausing after each strip to ask youngsters whether they remember what happened to the fox at that point in the story. Prompt students to come up with sound effects for the fox's antics. For example, the youngsters might say, "Thwack!" when the fox is hit by the rake or "Splash!" when it falls into the pond. Read the strips aloud again, encouraging students to add the appropriate sound effects.

Day 3

What Are They Saying?
Writing to expand the story

Gather a packet of sticky notes and turn to the first page of the book. Ask students what Rosie or the fox might be thinking. Then write their words on sticky notes and attach them to the page. Continue in the same way with different pages in the story, having students give the frogs, bird, and goat thoughts as well. Then read the story aloud, incorporating your little one's additional text.

It's nice outside today.

I'll get Rosie when she walks by.

This pond is really cold!

Day 4

Moving Along
Dramatizing a story

Have each youngster attach craft feathers to a simple hen cutout. Then have her attach a craft stick to the cutout to make a puppet. Place sentence strips with the story text on them in your pocket chart. As you read the strips, encourage youngsters to move their puppets to pantomime Rosie's actions.

Day 5

What Happened?
Retelling the story

Cut out a copy of the cards on page 166. Laminate them for durability and ready them for flannelboard use. Have youngsters help you attach the cards to the board in order. Then prompt youngsters to say the words of the story as they point to each appropriate card. Place the cards and the board in a center for independent retellings.

©The Mailbox® • TEC41045 • Oct./Nov. 2009

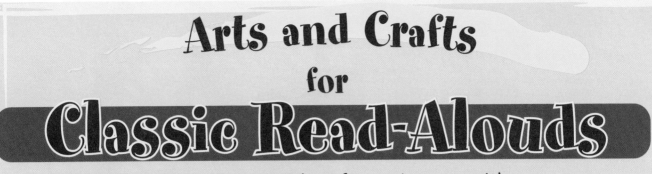

Arts and Crafts
for
Classic Read-Alouds

These creative arts-and-crafts projects go with your youngsters' favorite classic stories!

ideas contributed by Janet Boyce, Cokato, MN

Corduroy

Written and illustrated by Don Freeman

Here's an adorable craft that resembles Corduroy's button! To make one, place a piece of corrugated cardboard under a sheet of light colored construction paper. Rub the side of an unwrapped crayon on the paper. Color a small paper plate. Punch four holes in the plate, as shown, and then thread a length of yarn through the holes. Glue the plate to the prepared paper.

Jamberry

Written and illustrated by Bruce Degen

The beautiful berries in this process-art idea are reminiscent of the berries in *Jamberry*! Gather red, purple, and blue food coloring. Use the food coloring to tint individual containers of clear glue. Place an eyedropper next to each container. Use the eyedroppers to squeeze drops of colorful glue onto a sheet of paper. The result is a beautiful bunch of berries!

If You Give a Moose a Muffin

Written by Laura Numeroff
Illustrated by Felicia Bond

What kind of muffin would a moose enjoy most? Well, no one really knows, but this blueberry swirl muffin is sure to be a popular choice! Place small dollops of blue and white paint on a brown construction paper muffin cutout (pattern on page 169). Then use a plastic spoon to swirl the paint as desired. No moose could resist this muffin!

Goodnight Moon

Written by Margaret Wise Brown
Illustrated by Clement Hurd

This moon and window are reminiscent of the ones in the story! Attach a blue rectangle cutout to a 9" x 12" sheet of green construction paper. Crumple a white cupcake liner (moon), uncrumple it, and then glue the moon to the paper. Dot glue around the moon and then sprinkle glitter on the glue. Finally, attach red construction paper strips to the project so they resemble a window frame.

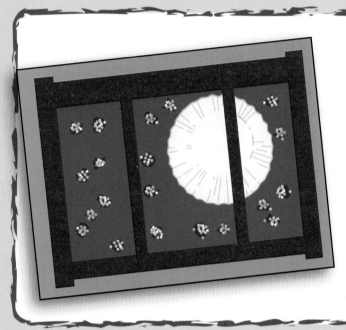

Where the Wild Things Are

Written and illustrated by Maurice Sendak

The horns, the claws, the teeth—this collage contains the best parts of the wild things! In advance, prepare containers of macaroni (claws), small construction paper triangles (teeth), and large construction paper triangles (horns). Glue the items to a sheet of colorful construction paper to make a wild collage!

Muffin Pattern

Use with *"If You Give a Moose a Muffin"* on page 168.

TEC41046

Fox in Socks

Where would a fox wear socks in a box with clocks? Why, in Dr. Seuss's rhythmic rhyming world, of course. But be careful reading this tricky fox's word play—after twisting through this tale, your tongue just may be numb.

ideas contributed by Ada Goren, Winston-Salem, NC

Twisted Tongues
Developing an interest in the story

Before reading this Seuss classic, teach youngsters a traditional tongue twister, such as "She sells seashells by the seashore." Invite volunteers to say the tongue twister. Explain that tongue twisters have similar sounds and those sounds make them difficult to say. Then tell them that you have a book that is full of tongue twisters. To begin the story, read aloud the message on the front cover and show students the warning page at the beginning of the book.

In the Box
Rhyming pictures

Fox certainly enjoys finding words that rhyme with *box.* Your youngsters will enjoy it too with this simple activity! Cut apart a copy of the cards on page 172. Scatter the cards facedown near a box. Then invite a volunteer to take a card and name the picture on it. If the name rhymes with *box,* have him place the card in the box. If it doesn't, direct him to set the card aside. Continue with the remaining cards.

Fun Favorites
Graphing

With this activity, youngsters identify their favorite sections of the book. For each child, personalize a sock cutout (pattern on page 172). Then draw a simple representation of each section of the book on separate cards. Label the cards and place them on a floor graph. Revisit the sections of the book. Then have each child place his sock on the graph to show his favorite section. Lead little ones in counting and comparing the socks in each column.

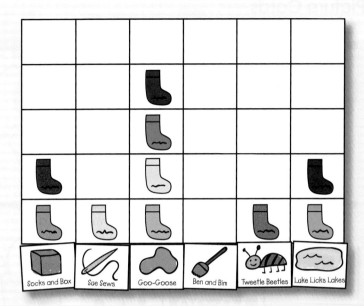

Socks and Box	Sue Sews	Goo-Goose	Ben and Bim	Tweetle Beetles	Lake Licks Lakes

Beetle Book
Phoneme manipulation

Revisit the pages about tweetle beetles with your youngsters. Then invite each child to draw a beetle of her own design on a sheet of paper. Prompt her to name the beetle using a rhyming word. Then have her manipulate the word *beetle* again to create the sound her beetle will make. Write a sentence like the one shown, using the child's words. Bind the pages together to make a class book and then share the book with youngsters.

Mae's sweetle beetle says, "Veetle, veetle!"

Snazzy Socks
Responding to a story through art

Fox needs some flashier socks than the plain old blue ones he wears in the story. Give each child two sock cutouts (pattern on page 172) and access to a variety of art materials. Invite her to decorate Fox's new socks as desired. Then display the pairs of socks on a board prepared like the one shown.

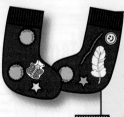

We made socks to put on Fox
After reading Fox in Socks.
These Fox socks aren't plain and blue, sir.
They are new and fun to view, sir!

Chicka Chicka Boom Boom

Written by Bill Martin Jr. and John Archambault
Illustrated by Lois Ehlert

The mischievous letters of the alphabet decide to congregate at the top of the coconut tree, which bends lower and lower until all the little letters end up in a pile on the ground. The letters wiggle free, but this beloved story doesn't end there!

Handprint Trees

Developing fine-motor skills

These adorable projects are a nifty way to commemorate a read-aloud of this classic story! Have each youngster paint a brown tree trunk on a sheet of construction paper. Then have him make two green handprints (with thumbs facing downward) above the trunk. Invite him to glue brown pom-pom coconuts to the tree. Then have him glue a copy of the chant shown to the project.

Jennie Jensen, North Cedar Elementary, Lowden, IA

Adam

Chicka, chicka, look at me.
My handprints made this coconut tree!

Make a Match

Matching uppercase letters to lowercase letters

Make a simple coconut tree from bulletin board paper and place it on your floor. Gather uppercase letter cards so there is a different card for each child and matching lowercase letter cards. Give a lowercase letter card to each child. Then reread the story, encouraging each child to place his card on the tree when his letter is mentioned. After the story, give each child a different uppercase letter card. Then encourage each youngster, in turn, to place his card on top of the matching lowercase letter.

Alison Craig, Briarwood Christian School, Birmingham, AL

Coconut Count

Identifying numbers, counting

Carry this story theme into your math center with a simple and tasty activity! Make a class supply of mats from page 178 and place them at a center along with a set of number cards and a supply of chocolate puffed cereal (coconuts). A child takes a coconut tree and a small cup of coconuts. If desired, he colors his mat. Then he places the cards facedown. He turns over a card and identifies the number. He counts that number of coconuts and places them on his tree. He continues in the same way until he runs out of coconuts. Then he nibbles on his manipulatives!

Jennie Jensen, North Cedar Elementary, Lowden, IA

Shake the Coconuts

Gross-motor skills

In advance, make several craft foam circle cutouts (coconuts) and place them on a bedsheet (or parachute). Have youngsters grab the edges of the sheet and shake it as you lead them in chanting the first verse of the rhyme below. After youngsters shake all the coconuts off the sheet, encourage them to pick up the coconuts and place them back on the sheet as they chant the final verse.

Shake, shake, shake the coconuts.
Shake, shake, shake the coconuts.
Shake, shake, shake the coconuts.
Watch those coconuts drop. Plop! Plop!

Find, find, find the coconuts.
Find, find, find the coconuts.
Find, find, find the coconuts.
Pick those coconuts up. Yup! Yup!

Jennie Jensen

What Happened?

Retelling the story

Supply simple props for youngsters to use to retell this fun story! Attach a coconut tree cutout to a cookie sheet. Then place the sheet at a center along with magnetic letters and a copy of the book. Encourage students to "read" the book, placing and removing magnetic letters to retell the story.

Michelle Freed, Peru, NE

©The Mailbox® • TEC41049 • June/July 2010

178   THE MAILBOX   **Note to the teacher:** Use with "Coconut Count" on page 177.

CENTER UNITS

My Classmates and Me Centers

Youngsters celebrate themselves and their classmates with this nifty selection of center ideas just perfect for the beginning of the school year!

Colorful Initials
Literacy Center

Make an initial page for each child and place it at a center with a variety of colorful craft items. Each student visits the center and finds his initial page. He traces the letter with his finger. Then he chooses craft items in his favorite color and attaches them to his initial.

On the Bus
Math Center

In advance, cut out a square head shot photo for each child. Laminate the photos for durability. Then make a large simple bus cutout with a class supply of windows. If desired, attach your own photo to the driver's window. Place the bus at a center along with the photos and a large foam die. A child rolls the die and counts to that number. Then he counts out the same number of photos and places them on the bus. He continues until he and all his classmates are on the bus!

Moldable Me!
Play Dough Center

Place a supply of colorful play dough at a center along with rolling pins and people cookie cutters in a variety of sizes. Also provide a laminated photo of each student. A youngster rolls out dough and cuts out people shapes. Then she decorates them to resemble her classmates or herself.

Photogenic Classmates
Flannelboard Center

Laminate a photo of each child; then attach the hook side of an adhesive Velcro fastener to the back of each cutout. Place the cutouts near your flannelboard with several other flannelboard cutouts. A youngster visits the center and places the photos and shapes of his choosing on the board. After he is satisfied with his work, he tells a story about his flannelboard arrangement.

Iris Burris, Zion Lutheran School, Fallbrook, CA

... and the big grey doggy ran from Jake...

Gorgeous Cakes
Art Center

Make a copy of the cake cutout on page 182 for each child and label the cutout with her name and birthdate. Place the cakes at your art center with an assortment of decorating supplies. A youngster visits the center, locates her cake, and then decorates it using materials of her choosing. If desired, use metal rings to bind the cakes between two covers and then title the project "Our Class Birthday Book."

Carole Watkins, Crown Point, IN

Lauren
April 4, 2005

Cake Pattern

Use with "Gorgeous Cakes" on page 181.

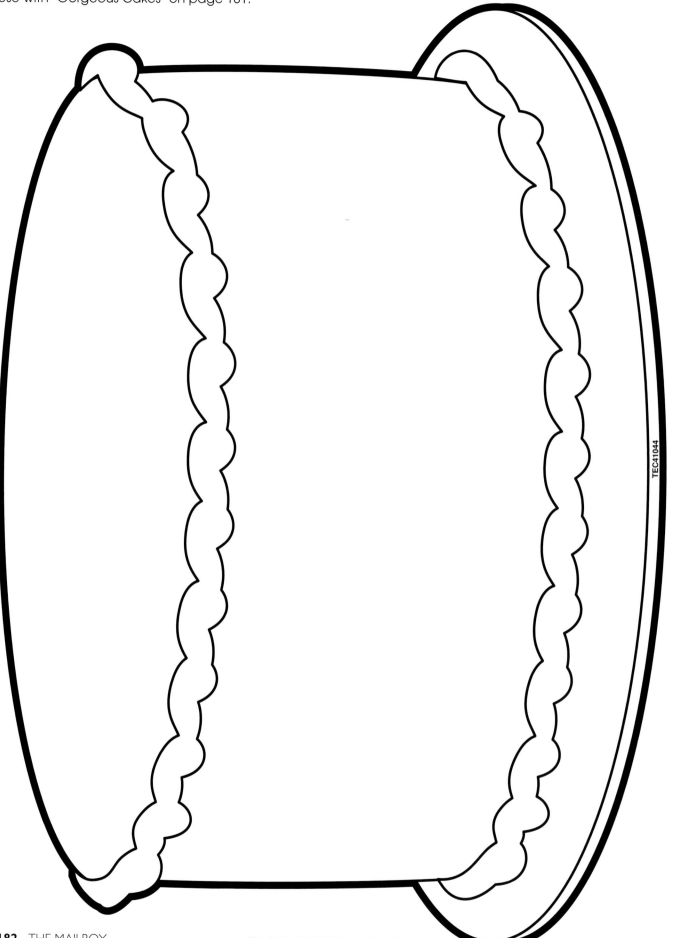

TEC41044

Black and Orange Centers

Celebrate these spooky fall colors with a selection of adorable center ideas!

Piercing Pumpkins
Fine-Motor Area

Place at a table several pumpkins, large wood screws, screwdrivers, toy hammers, and safety goggles. A child visits the center and dons a pair of safety goggles. He uses a hammer to tap the tip of a screw into the pumpkin flesh. Then he uses a screwdriver to screw the wood screw into the pumpkin.

Susan Ehrhardt
St. Paul Nursery School
Cincinnati, OH

Web Full of Spiders
Gross-Motor Area

Wrap yarn around a plastic hoop toy so it resembles a spiderweb, taping the yarn in place as needed. Place the web on the floor and make a tape line several feet from the web. Provide a container of plastic spiders (or large black pom-poms). A child stands behind the line and tries to toss each spider onto the web. Then she counts aloud the spiders that landed on the web.

Norinne Weeks
Carrillo Elementary
Houston, TX

Halloween Kitty
Writing Center

What would this cat do on Halloween? No doubt your youngsters will be eager to tell you with this adorable project! For each child, cut out a black construction paper cat body and tail. Then place the cutouts at a center along with green glitter for eyes, pieces of white rickrack for whiskers, and glue. A child uses the items to make a cat similar to the one shown. Then she dictates what her cat would do on Halloween night. Use a white crayon or silver marker to write her words on her cat.

Kathy Cole, Troy Grade School, Troy, KS

My cat will scare trick-or-treaters on Halloween!

Bats and Caves
Literacy Center

Youngsters practice letter matching and formation with this tactile idea! Label several pairs of bat and cave cutouts (patterns on page 185) with matching letters; then squeeze glue over each letter. (If desired, attach mini wiggle eyes to each bat.) After the glue is dry, sort the bats and caves and spread each set faceup on your floor. A child chooses a bat and traces the letter using her index finger. She "flies" the bat to the caves, finds the matching cave, and traces the letter on it in the same way. Then she places the pair to the side.

Tricia Kylene Brown, Bowling Green, KY

Comfy Pumpkin
Reading Center

Cut a door in a large appliance box. Paint the box orange so it resembles a pumpkin; then attach a large paper stem and vines to the top. Place soft pillows, a battery-operated camping lamp, and theme-related books in the box. What a relaxing place to look at books!

Halloween Story

Halloween

TEC41045

TEC41045

Home and Family

Centers

ideas contributed by Roxanne LaBell Dearman,
NC Early Intervention Program for Children Who
Are Deaf or Hard of Hearing, Charlotte, NC

Family Chores

Sensory Center

Fill two plastic tubs with water; then add lemon-scented dish detergent to one tub to make it sudsy. Add to the sudsy water items such as plastic dinnerware, a sponge, and a pot scrubber. Place a dish rack and a dish towel nearby. Youngsters visit the center and pretend to be family members doing the dishes together.

Photo Frame

Art Center

Place a supply of house-shaped tagboard frames in your art center along with paper sized to fit the frames. A youngster draws a picture of her family on the paper and then glues the picture facedown to the frame. Then she turns the frame over and decorates it as desired.

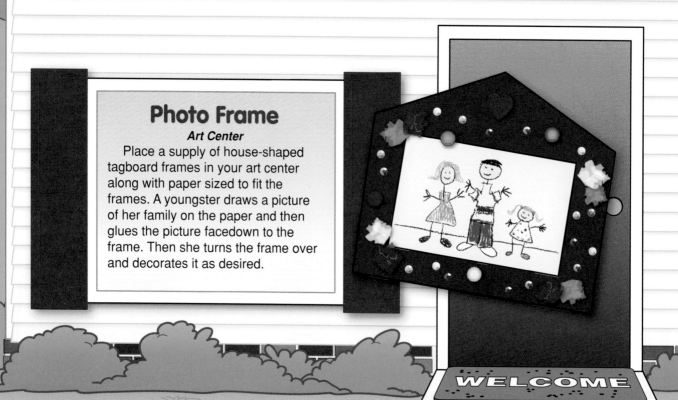

WELCOME

High-Five Fun
Writing Center
Station an adult helper at a table and provide a shallow pan of paint. A child makes a handprint on a sheet of paper. Then the helper has the child name five things he enjoys doing with his family as she writes each item above a different finger.

Going to the beach

Reading a bedtime story with Daddy

Going to the park with Grandpa

Playing tag with my brother

Making a cake with Mommy

Stephen

Shopping List
Literacy Center
Provide grocery store circulars and a class supply of copies of page 188. A student writes her name on a grocery list. Then she looks through the circulars, cuts out pictures of items to put on her family shopping list, and glues the pictures to the paper. When she is finished, she names the items on her list aloud.

Meghan 's Family
Grocery List

Cola

MILK

ICE CREAM

PIZZA

Bear Families
Math Center
To prepare for this sorting activity, fill a small bowl with bear-shaped cookies in two different colors. Set out two construction paper copies of the cottage on page 189; then place a different-colored bear on each cottage door. A youngster visits the center and sorts the bears into their matching families. When he is finished, he nibbles on a separate cup of bear cookies set aside for a snack.

Jennifer Gemar, Tripp-Delmont Schools, Tripp, SD

Cozy Quilt Centers

ideas contributed by Lucia Kemp Henry, Fallon, NV

Designer Squares
Art Center

Combine these individual projects into a lovely quilt display! Precut a supply of 8-inch tagboard squares. Also provide scraps of seasonal gift wrap, scissors, glue sticks, and markers. A child cuts or tears the paper scraps and glues the pieces to a square. He uses a marker to draw stitch lines and then trims any excess paper from the edges of the square.

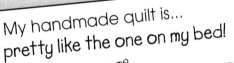

GLUE

My handmade quilt is... pretty like the one on my bed!

Pretty Patchwork
Writing Center

In advance, cut a supply of 2-inch squares from colorful scrapbook paper. Also make a copy of page 192 for each child and provide crayons and glue. A youngster draws facial details and hair on the head outline so it resembles herself and colors the page as desired. Then she glues a square to each quilt space on her paper. When her quilt is finished, she dictates words to complete the prompt.

Lovely Letters
Literacy Center

For this letter-matching activity, decorate pairs of construction paper squares (quilt squares) with a simple border and then label each pair with matching letters. Store the squares in a container and provide a large sheet of construction paper programmed as shown. A student picks a quilt square, finds the square with the matching letter, and then places the pair side by side on the paper. He continues until the quilt is complete.

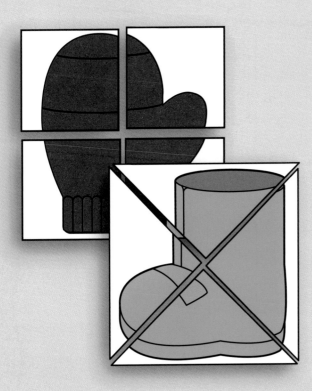

Winter Handiwork
Puzzle Center

To make a quilt-patch puzzle, glue a winter-related cutout—such as a mitten, boot, hat, or snowflake—to a construction paper square. Cut the square into four equal pieces and store the pieces in a resealable plastic bag. Make several puzzles in this way. A child removes the pieces from a bag and completes the quilt patch puzzle. **For an added challenge,** put the pieces for two or more puzzles in a single bag!

Shapely Designs
Math Center

Students develop shape matching and shape identification skills with this idea! Make several quilt block templates by tracing various shape manipulatives onto tagboard squares as shown. Provide a supply of colorful shapes. A child decorates a quilt block by placing matching shapes on a template, naming the shapes as she works.

My handmade quilt is...

Note to the teacher: Use with "Pretty Patchwork" on page 190.

Splendid Rain Centers!

How Many Raindrops?
Math Center

Students practice number identification and making sets with this idea. Set out a cloud-shaped cutout, number cards, and blue play dough. A child takes a card, identifies the number, and places the card on the cloud. Then she uses the play dough to make a corresponding number of raindrops below the cloud.

Rexann Roussel
Narrow Acres Preschool
Paulina, LA

Play Dough

5

Puddle Play
Gross-Motor Area

Attach several large felt puddle cutouts to the floor in an open area of the room. Provide rain gear—such as a raincoat, a poncho, or rubber boots—for youngsters to wear. A student puts on the rain gear and then uses a variety of gross-motor movements to engage in pretend puddle play.

Lisa Igou
Silbernagel Elementary
Dickinson, TX

Make It Rain
Fine-Motor Area

Little ones fine-tune their pincer grasps with this fun idea. Arrange plastic animals and plants in a shallow tub to create an outdoor scene. Provide a container of water and a supply of cotton balls. A youngster dips a cotton ball in the water and then squeezes the cotton ball over the props, pretending to make it rain.

Tricia Glenn
Providence Christian Academy
Georgetown, KY

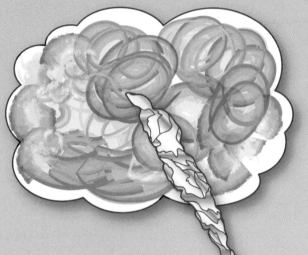

Lightning Storm
Art Center

Mix together two parts shaving cream and one part white glue; then tint the mixture gray. Set the mixture at a table along with cloud-shaped cutouts and aluminum foil. A child fingerpaints a cloud cutout with a thick layer of the mixture; then she crumples a piece of foil to form a lightning bolt and presses it onto the project.

Carmen Prada, Learning Unlimited, Bradenton, FL

When It Rains...
Writing Center

Make a copy of page 195 for each child and provide markers or crayons and a blue stamp pad. A student draws a picture of something he likes to do when it rains. Then he presses his fingertip on the ink pad and then onto the paper to fill the page with raindrops. When the page is complete, he dictates words to complete the prompt and writes his name on the line.

When it rains...
I pretend I am really big and I stomp in puddles.

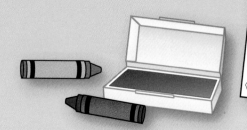

When it rains...

by _____

Note to the teacher: Use with "When It Rains…" on page 194.

Ice Cream Centers

Favorite Flavor

Sensory Center

Station an adult helper at a table. Set out disposable bowls, plastic spoons, two flavors of ice cream, and a copy of page 198 programmed with the two flavor choices. For each child, put a dollop of each flavor of ice cream in a bowl. A child eats the ice cream, savoring each flavor. Then he writes his name in the appropriate column to show which one he likes best.

Amy D'Agostino, Syracuse, NY

Which Flavor Is Your Favorite?

chocolate	strawberry
Julie	Amber
Marshall	Dion
Tony	Destiny
Nicole	
Ryan	

Ice Cream, Anyone?

Sand Table

Fill your sand table with very moist sand. Provide plastic bowls, plastic cups, ice cream scoops, mini pom-poms (sprinkles), medium-size red pom-poms (cherries), and plastic spoons. A youngster uses the kitchen props and sand to make ice cream cones and sundaes. Then she tops her treats with sprinkles and cherries.

"Scooper-duper" Hopscotch
Gross-Motor Area

Laminate several large bowl cutouts, each programmed with one or two construction paper ice cream scoops as shown. Attach the bowls to the floor, alternating the number of scoops. A child hops along the ice cream path, hopping on one or two feet to match the number of scoops. As he hops, he recites the chant shown.

I like ice cream;
Yes, I do!
One scoop, two scoops—
How about you?

Jennie Jensen, Clarence, IA
Shannon McCarthy-Bannon, St. Catherine Laboure, Glenview, IL

Single Scoops
Literacy Center

Cut apart the cards from the centerfold and sort the cone cards from the scoop cards. A student chooses a scoop card, identifies the letter, and tells whether it is uppercase or lowercase. Then she finds the ice cream cone with the matching letter and places the scoop above the cone. She continues until all the uppercase and lowercase letters are matched.

How Many Sprinkles?
Math Center

Set out a large construction paper ice cream cone. Provide number cards and a supply of colorful milk caps (sprinkles). A youngster takes a card and identifies the number. Then he counts aloud that number of sprinkles and puts them on the ice cream. When he is finished, he removes the sprinkles and repeats the activity using a different number card.

Which Flavor Is Your Favorite?

LITERACY UNITS

A Bushel of Print and Book Awareness

ideas contributed by Roxanne LaBell Dearman, Western NC Early Intervention Program for Children Who Are Deaf or Hard of Hearing Charlotte, NC

Print Around the Room

Understanding that print has meaning

Point out print in your classroom and attach a sticky-note flag to the print. Say, "These words tell me something." Then read the print aloud. Give a child a sticky-note flag and encourage her to find another example of print in the room. Read aloud the print or redirect her if she points to a series of numbers or other symbols. Then have her attach her flag to the print. Continue having students find and flag examples of print.

Block Center

That's My Favorite!

Expressing an opinion about a book

Have each child color and cut out a personalized copy of a bookworm from page 203. Laminate the worms for durability. Then place the bookworms in a container in your reading area. When a child visits the reading area and finds a particular book she enjoys, have her slip her bookworm into the book. (You may want to place library card pockets in your books to hold the bookworms.) From time to time, pull out a book and comment on the bookworm. "Why, this book must be Sarah's favorite!"

Jimmy

Tasty Options

Reading environmental print

Send home with each child a red paper plate and an instruction sheet similar to the one shown. After each child brings his plate back, bind the plates together with a metal ring. Then flip through the plates with your youngsters, encouraging them to read the different types of environmental print.

Dear Family,
    This little apple worm is tired of eating apples! Your youngster can provide other food options for it to enjoy. Please help your child cut familiar food labels from boxes and other food packages and then glue the labels onto the provided plate. Have him return the plate to school by September 15.

Thank you!
Ms. Dearman

Check This Out!

To evaluate youngsters' book knowledge, add page turner to your daily jobs. During storytime, have the page turner sit by your side. When you are finished reading a page, nod to the page turner and have her turn the page for you, noting whether she is confident that pages are turned from right to left.

Wonder Worm

Speaking to ask questions about a book

Bend a green pipe cleaner (worm) into a question mark. Show youngsters the storytime selection for the day. Then introduce the worm as a wonder worm. Tell students that you're holding the wonder worm because you're wondering about something. Say, "I wonder…" followed by something from the book you might have a question about based on the cover illustration. Model this process for other storytime selections throughout the week. When youngsters are comfortable with this process, give the wonder worm to a volunteer.

A Big Bookworm

Identifying the title, author, and illustrator

Make several circle cutouts and decorate one so it resembles a worm's head. Attach the head to your wall. When you read a book to your class, help students identify the title, author, and illustrator of the book. Explain that the author writes the words and the illustrator draws the pictures. Then write the title, author, and illustrator on a circle and have a student attach it behind the head to create a portion of the worm's body. Continue with each book you read throughout the year, and this worm will soon stretch all the way around the room!

Jamberry
Written and illustrated by Bruce Degen

Bear Snores On
Written by Karma Wilson
Illustrated by Jane Chapman

One red apple high in the tree,

I stretch up tall to try to see.

I reach up high—that apple's in sight.

I'll pick that apple and take a bite!

Wormy Pointer

Tracking print from left to right

Copy onto sentence strips the rhyme shown and then place them in your pocket chart. Wrap a green pipe cleaner around your index finger to make a special bookworm pointer. To begin, read aloud the rhyme from right to left as you follow the words with the worm. Then say, "Oh my goodness, this silly worm isn't reading in the right direction!" Have students guide the worm to read the poem correctly. Slip the worm off your finger and onto a child's finger and have him follow the rhyme as you read aloud. Continue with several volunteers.

Jennifer Rhine, Preschool Express, Millersville, PA

Bookworm Patterns
Use with "That's My Favorite!" on page 200.

THE MAILBOX **203**

TEC41044

TEC41044

Gobbling Good Phonological Awareness

ideas contributed by Ada Goren, Winston-Salem, NC

Shell. Bell.

Fine-Feathered Turkey

Identifying rhyming words

Attach a simple turkey body cutout to your board and make several colorful feather patterns. Say two words and encourage a child to identify whether the words rhyme. If they do, have him attach a feather to the turkey. If they don't, have him do nothing. Continue giving youngsters turns until each child has attached a feather to the turkey.

corn
turkey
feast
Thanksgiving
stuffing
Pilgrim
pie
gravy
cranberry
pumpkin
squash
potato

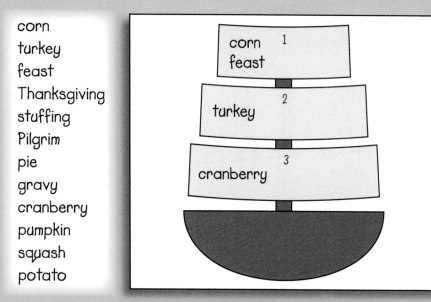

corn 1
feast
turkey 2
cranberry 3

Syllables on Sails

Clapping syllables

Draw on chart paper a ship with three sails. Number the sails. Then gather students and say a Thanksgiving-related word, such as one of the ones shown. Encourage youngsters to clap the syllables in the word and then identify the number of claps. Next, have a child identify which sail number corresponds with the number of syllables. Write the word on the sail. Then repeat the process with other words.

Favorite Foods

Manipulating phonemes

Cut from magazines pictures of favorite Thanksgiving foods and attach them to a large circle cutout (plate). Display the plate. Then tell students that the items on the plate are your favorite Thanksgiving foods. Introduce one of the foods by calling it a nonsense rhyming name, such as "luffing" instead of "stuffing." No doubt your youngsters will giggle and immediately correct your mistake! Continue in the same way with each remaining food item.

Mouthwatering Verse

Reciting rhyming chants

Lead youngsters in reciting this cute little chant several times, encouraging them to tap a steady beat on different parts of their bodies for each repetition.

Mashed potatoes, turkey, stuffing,
Green beans, gravy, and corn muffin.
Pumpkin pie is such a treat
With some whipped cream—oh so sweet.

Same-Sounds Stuffing

Matching beginning sounds

Cut out a copy of the cards on page 207 and a copy of the turkey pattern at the top of page 208. Place the cards in your pocket chart with the backs facing outward. Attach the turkey to a wall. Encourage a child to choose two cards from the pocket chart and say the names of the pictures. If the beginning sounds match, have her attach the cards to the turkey. If they do not, prompt her to place the cards back in the pocket chart. Continue until the turkey has been "stuffed" with the matching pairs.

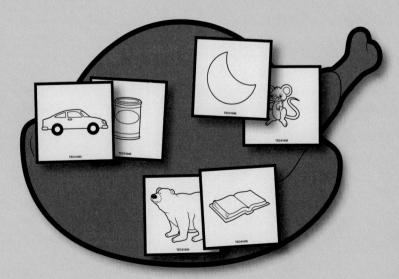

Tap the Turkey
Identifying beginning sound /t/

Give each child a copy of the turkey from page 208 and have him place the turkey in front of him on the floor. Explain that the word *turkey* begins with /t/. Then say, "/t/, /t/, table." Since *table* begins with /t/, prompt students to say, "Tap the turkey!" and then encourage youngsters to tap the turkey cutout with their fingers. Continue the game with other words, only prompting youngsters to tap the turkey when the word begins with /t/.

Robin Reisdorf, Kids' Safari Learning Center, Cottage Grove, WI

Tap the turkey!

Saucy Sentences
Segmenting a sentence into words

Give each youngster in a small group a red puddle cutout (cranberry sauce) and several red pom-poms (cranberries). Say a Thanksgiving-related sentence, such as "I like turkey." Prompt each child to place one cranberry in his sauce for each word in the sentence. Then have him count the cranberries. After he removes the cranberries, continue with a new sentence.

Wonderful Wordplay
Manipulating phonemes

Gather a few Thanksgiving-related pictures from newspapers or magazines. Hold up a picture and say the name of the item and then a rhyming nonsense word, such as "Turkey. Burkey." Give the picture to a child and encourage him to repeat the process, saying the real word and a new nonsense word. Continue with several youngsters and then start the activity again with a new picture.

TEC41045

TEC41045

TEC41045

TEC41045

TEC41045

TEC41045

TEC41045

TEC41045

TEC41045

TEC41045

TEC41045

TEC41045

Cooked Turkey Pattern
Use with "Same-Sounds Stuffing" on page 205.

Turkey Pattern
Use with "Tap the Turkey" on page 206.

A Flurry of Literacy Ideas!

Throwing Snowballs
Sorting uppercase and lowercase letters
Label foam balls (snowballs) with either an uppercase letter or a lowercase letter. Store the balls in a container at a center along with a pair of mittens. Several feet away, place two empty boxes labeled as shown. A little one puts on the mittens, takes a ball, and tosses it in the appropriate box. He continues with each remaining ball.

Jennie Jensen, North Cedar Elementary, Lowden, IA

Uppercase Letters
ABC

Lowercase Letters
abc

On the Bus!
Letter-sound association
This toe-tapping tune reinforces the beginning sounds of students' names. Lead little ones in singing the song, inserting a child's name and corresponding beginning sound when appropriate. Then repeat the song with other students' names as time allows.

(sung to the tune of "The Wheels on the Bus")

Oh, let's play a sound game with our names,
With our names, with our names.
Let's play a sound game with our names.
Let's try [Child's name]!
[Child's name] starts with [sound, sound, sound],
[Sound, sound, sound], [sound, sound, sound].
[Child's name] starts with [sound, sound, sound].
Whose name is next?

Stephanie Angel, LBJ Elementary, Jackson, KY

Give a Gift

Recognizing the letter G

Decorate a sheet of poster board so that it looks like a gift. Place the poster board at a center along with a gift bag containing a set of letter cards—some labeled with *G*s and a few labeled with different letters. Tell students that the recipient of this gift wants only *G*s. A child picks a card from the bag. If the card is programmed with a *G,* she places it on the gift. If it is not, she sets it aside. She continues in the same manner with each remaining card.

Michelle Brady
Our Lady of the Holy Rosary School
Gardner, MA

Candy Cane

Forming the letter J

For this mouthwatering project, give each child a sheet of paper labeled with a large *J.* Encourage each student to trace the letter with her finger and say the letter's name. Have her trim strips of red and white paper into small squares and then glue the squares to the letter *J* in an *AB* pattern. When each child is finished, have her turn her paper upside down to see how her completed project resembles a candy cane!

Pam Dudek, Holy Cross Lutheran Preschool
Spring Hill, FL

Letter Big Book

Letter-sound association

Invite students to assist you in making this simple big book. Write a letter on a large sheet of paper. Invite a youngster to identify the letter and make its sound. Continue in this manner with other letters. When a desired number of pages are complete, bind the pages between two tagboard covers. Read the completed book aloud to students and then place it in your reading area.

Mary Davis
Keokuk Christian Academy
Keokuk, IA

B.

Typing Letters
Matching letters
Set out an old computer keyboard. Then make letter sequence cards. A youngster takes a sequence card and types the letters on the keyboard in order. What a terrific typist!

Mary Davis
Keokuk Christian Academy
Keokuk, IA

T K L O M

Bag Booklet
Writing a caption
Students add captions to magazine pictures to make this creative booklet. Cut a supply of pictures from magazines. Ask each child to choose a picture and describe it. Write his words on a 3" x 5" card and then attach the card to his picture. Insert each picture into a large resealable plastic bag, keeping the opening on the right. Stack the bags between two construction paper covers and staple the stack on the left edge to make a booklet.

Dorothy McAlister
Desert Palms Elementary
Glendale, AZ

The boy is playing with his Daddy. They are playing in the snow. They are having fun.

Trim the Tree
Participating in a rhyme
Cut out colorful copies of the star patterns from page 213 and prepare them for flannelboard use. Randomly place the stars on a tabletop. Place a large felt evergreen tree on your flannelboard. Read aloud the first two lines of the text shown. Then pause; have a child find a yellow star and place it on the tree. Continue with the next two lines; then pause and have a child place a blue star on the tree. Continue in the same way with each of the remaining stars.

Devin Manning
Machesney Park, IL

Evergreen tree, evergreen tree, what do you see?
I see a yellow star looking at me.
Yellow star, yellow star, what do you see?
I see a blue star looking at me!

Sweet Letters

Sweet Letters
Letter formation

These letters look good enough to eat! Give each child a brown letter cutout. Invite each child to trace the letter with his finger and say its name. Then have him squeeze a line of glue (icing) on the letter. Encourage him to add craft items to the letter so it resembles decorated gingerbread. If desired, display the finished projects with a decorated gingerbread house cutout and the title shown.

Phyllis Prestridge, West Amory Elementary, Amory, MS

Holiday Stories
Writing

Recycled holiday cards are perfect for jump-starting youngsters' writing. Cut the pictures from a supply of holiday cards and invite each youngster to choose one. Have each child glue her picture near the top of a sheet of construction paper. Then have her dictate a story about the picture for you to write below it.

Marie E. Cecchini
West Dundee, IL

This tree is beautiful. There are lots of presents under the tree. It is a nice tree.

In the News
Letter recognition

Give each child in a small group a list of letters and a highlighter. Also provide a stack of newspapers. Invite each child to look through the newspapers to find his listed letters. When he finds a letter, have him circle it in the newspaper and cross it off his list. Each child continues until he has found each of his assigned letters.

Andrea Henderson
Jefferson Brethren Preschool
Goshen, IN

NEWS & RECORD

Supreme Court supports ban

Vote on land gets principal to pass notes

U.S. will continue flights

Index

First female mayors to be elected in county

Letter List

P B M O K A J

TEC41046

TEC41046

TEC41046

TEC41046

Getting Ready to Write

These helpful tips and activities are sure to be just "write" for your little ones.

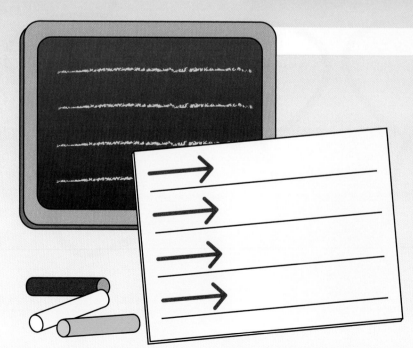

Squirt!

Developing fine-motor skills

This easy-to-prepare idea is a fabulous way to strengthen muscles needed for writing! Use chalk to write letters on the pavement. Then give youngsters squirt bottles of water and encourage them to squirt water over the letters.

Karen Eiben
The Learning House Preschool
La Salle, IL

The Right Direction

Writing from left to right

Cut parallel slits in pieces of craft foam and use a permanent marker to draw arrows as shown. Place the craft foam pieces at a center along with small chalkboards (or sheets of black paper) and chalk in a variety of colors. A child places the craft foam over a chalkboard and then inserts chalk in the left side of one of the slits. He draws a line from the left to right, following the slit across the craft foam. He repeats the process with the remaining slits and different colors of chalk.

Theresa Eumurian
Vineyard Christian Preschool
Anaheim, CA

Go to page 217 for a fun reproducible activity to help your little writers develop their fine-motor skills!

Word Cards

Dictating information

These word rings are sure to be popular with your little ones. Place index cards at a table and station an adult nearby. Whenever a child thinks of a word she would like to see, she dictates it for the adult to write on a card. The child illustrates the word. Then she hole-punches the card, with help, and slides it onto a metal ring. Students continue to add word cards to their rings throughout the school year.

Stephanie Seto and Christina Sioss, P.S. 105, Brooklyn, NY

Go Glue!

Writing

Pour white glue in a resealable plastic bag. Remove any air from the bag and seal it, reinforcing the closure with tape. A youngster places the bag atop a sheet of colorful paper. Then she uses her finger to write on the bag. The colored paper shows through where her finger has moved the glue. It looks magical!

Cheryl Smith, Smith Academy, Richland, WA

From Large to Small

Forming letters

This tip will help your littlest preschoolers write their names. Use sidewalk chalk to write a child's name on the pavement. Then have the youngster use a large toy truck to trace the letters. When a child can do that comfortably, write his name on a large sheet of paper and encourage him to trace it with a toy car. Then have him trace his name with a crayon.

Dawn Smith, Dawn's Family Daycare, Wrentham, MA

Let's Trace!

Writing

Draw letters on a sheet of paper and attach the paper to a table. Place an acrylic plastic sheet (available in home improvement stores) atop the paper. Then place dry-erase markers at the table. A child traces the letters on the acrylic plastic sheet. After he admires his work, he wipes off the markings.

Mindy Robinson, Small Scholars Preschool, Plymouth, MA

A Tracking Chant

Tracking print from top to bottom and left to right

Lead youngsters in this simple but snappy action chant!

When we read	Pretend to open a book.
And when we write,	Pretend to write on palm.
We do it top to bottom	Point up and then down.
And left to right.	Point to the left and then move right.

Deborah Jackson
Glyndon Co-op Preschool Program
Reisterstown, MD

Pencil Stars

Developing the correct pencil grip

To help youngsters hold their pencils in the correct location, attach a star sticker to each pencil approximately one inch from the point. A youngster will immediately look for the star when he picks up a pencil. Now students' little fingers won't be too close to the middle or end of their pencils when they write!

Marilyn Horsley
Valley View United Methodist Preschool
Overland Park, KS

Lots of Love

Note to the teacher: Have each child trace the hearts on a copy of this page. Then encourage her to color the page as desired.

Let's Learn About
Letters and Sounds!

These letter and sound ideas are packed with learning fun!

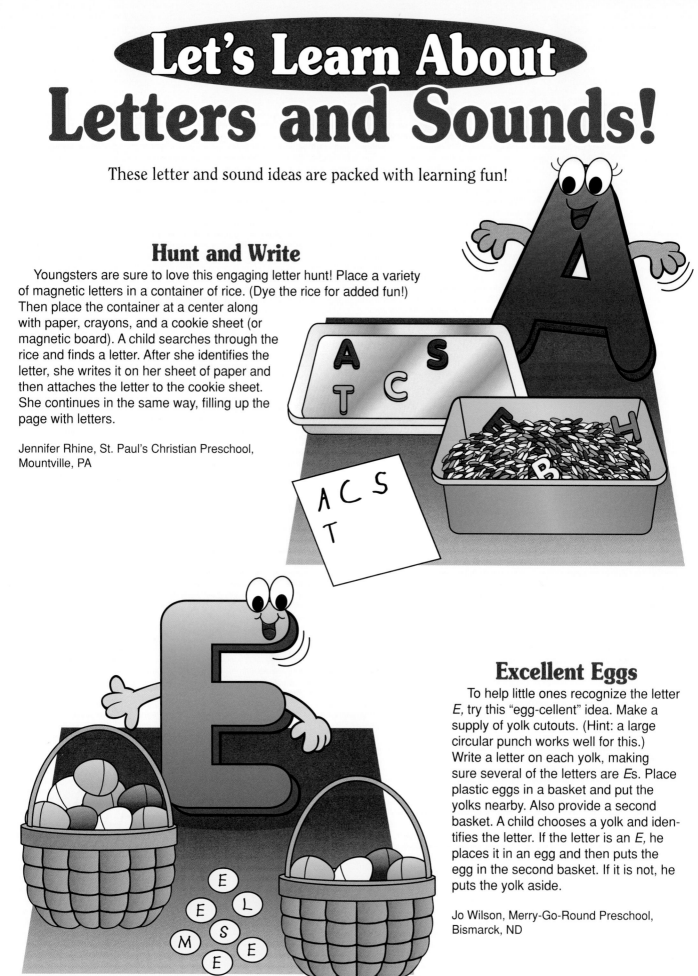

Hunt and Write

Youngsters are sure to love this engaging letter hunt! Place a variety of magnetic letters in a container of rice. (Dye the rice for added fun!) Then place the container at a center along with paper, crayons, and a cookie sheet (or magnetic board). A child searches through the rice and finds a letter. After she identifies the letter, she writes it on her sheet of paper and then attaches the letter to the cookie sheet. She continues in the same way, filling up the page with letters.

Jennifer Rhine, St. Paul's Christian Preschool, Mountville, PA

Excellent Eggs

To help little ones recognize the letter *E,* try this "egg-cellent" idea. Make a supply of yolk cutouts. (Hint: a large circular punch works well for this.) Write a letter on each yolk, making sure several of the letters are *E*s. Place plastic eggs in a basket and put the yolks nearby. Also provide a second basket. A child chooses a yolk and identifies the letter. If the letter is an *E,* he places it in an egg and then puts the egg in the second basket. If it is not, he puts the yolk aside.

Jo Wilson, Merry-Go-Round Preschool, Bismarck, ND

Different Lines

Make a chart with the headings shown. Place a supply of letter cards in a bag. Have a child remove a card from the bag. Then help him name the letter and identify whether it has straight lines, curved lines, or both types of lines. Help him tape the card in the corresponding column. Continue in the same way, having different youngsters choose cards from the bag.

Amber Dingman
Play 'n' Learn Family Childcare and Preschool
Sterling, IL

Straight	Curved	Both
L	O	G
Y K	S	R
W		P

Will It Fit?

This activity helps reinforce matching letter sounds and encourages youngsters to think about size comparisons. Show youngsters a vase. Then ask them whether they think a violin would fit in the vase. After they share and discuss their answers, ask them if they think a valentine would fit in the vase. Continue with the words *vegetable, van,* and *vacuum.* Then prompt students to name the sound at the beginning of the words. Play similar rounds of this game with the containers and words listed.

Containers and Words
can: *cat, cow, car, candy*
bowl: *bat, bed, bee, bird*
purse: *piano, pear, pizza, pin*
mug: *mop, moon, mushroom, mouse*
jar: *jam, jeep, jet, jacket*
wagon: *whale, watermelon, wig, worm*

Clare Cox, Homer Davis Elementary, Tucson, AZ

Banana Crème Pie

Label several yellow bottle caps (banana slices) with different letters, including many with the letter *B.* Place the banana slices in a bag. Put cotton balls in a pie tin so they resemble crème. To begin, have a child choose a banana slice and name the letter and its sound. If the slice has a *B* on it, encourage her to say, "/b/, /b/, banana," and then have her place the slice on the pie. If the slice doesn't have a letter *B,* have her set it aside.

Lara Cropsey, Greer, SC

A "T" Party

Spotlight the letter *T* with a special party! Encourage youngsters to bring a teddy bear from home for this special *T* party. Then have the teddies join youngsters as they decorate *T* cutouts with pieces of tinsel and have tacos as a special treat! What a fun way to celebrate this letter!

Susan Norton, Busy Bee Preschool, Thatcher, AZ

Check This Out!

When Donna Olp of St. Gregory the Great School, South Euclid, Ohio, has her little ones practice writing letters in the air, she concludes the activity with something special that engages youngsters' imaginations. She prompts her little ones to blow the invisible letters up to the ceiling so youngsters don't keep bumping into them throughout the day. What a great way to make an educational idea truly fun!

Letter Hunt

Hide die-cut letters around your room. Then give two children papers naming all the hidden letters. Also give them play walkie-talkies or cell phones. Encourage youngsters to search for the letters, marking each letter found on their papers. Prompt the partners to keep in contact by "radioing" each other to alert each other of each new find.

Jessica Strength, Walnut Ridge Baptist, Mansfield, TX

Literacy FUN

Here's a splendid selection of literacy ideas just perfect for any time throughout the school year!

Alphabet I Spy

Recognizing letter sounds

This simple activity requires only a pointer and an alphabet display! Say to students, "I spy a letter that says /m/." Then give a child a special pointer and prompt him to point to the appropriate letter on the alphabet display. Continue in the same way with different letters and volunteers.

Sami Pollard
Paradise, TX

Message in a Bottle

Writing

Remove the labels from several plastic bottles and place the bottles near your water table along with paper and crayons. Explain to youngsters that a person who is stuck on an island might write a note, put it in a bottle, and place it in the water with the hope that people will find it and save him. A youngster visits the center and writes a letter on a sheet of paper. Then she rolls it up and places it in a bottle. After she secures the cap, she floats the bottle in the water table.

Stacy Baker
Early Childhood Center
Hudson, OH

A Letter Pool

Identifying letters

To prepare for this activity, scatter letter cards on your floor. Tell students to pretend that the floor is a pool. Then have everyone jump in and "swim" to a letter. Each child picks up a card and then "climbs" out of the pool. Have each child identify the letter he found in the pool. Then encourage students to jump in and find other letters. To add a fun twist to the activity, have youngsters stop and pretend to float when you say, "Float!" or announce that there is a letter shark in the area and encourage them to get their letters very quickly!

Michele Sears, Northeast R-IV School, Cairo, MO

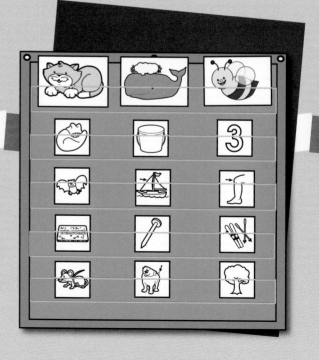

Toss and Name

Identifying environmental print

Collect food boxes, wrappers, and advertisements with appropriate environmental print. Then trim the environmental print as needed and attach it to a length of bulletin board paper. Place the paper on your floor and put a tape line several feet away. Place several beanbags near the tape line. A child tosses a beanbag. When she retrieves the beanbag, she identifies the environmental print it landed on.

Evon Rose Todd, Mid Cities Head Start, Euless, TX

Splendid Sort

Identifying rhyming pictures

This activity can be used in a pocket chart for circle time or in a center for individual practice! Cut apart a copy of the cards on pages 223 and 224. Place the header cards in the top of your pocket chart. (For a center, lightly tape them to a tabletop.) Have youngsters sort the picture cards below the headers with which they rhyme.

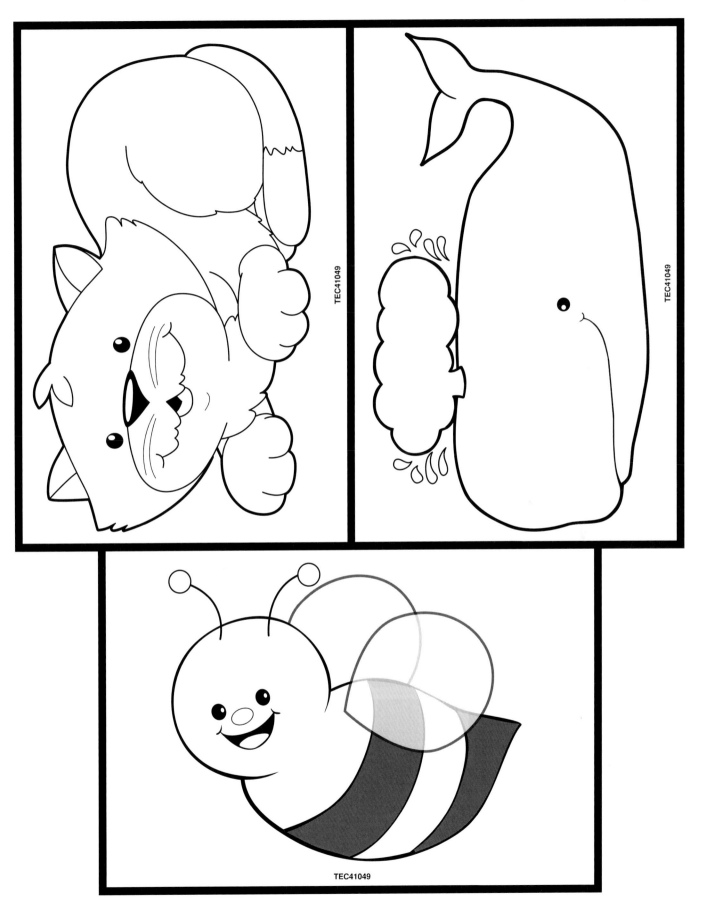

TEC41049

TEC41049

TEC41049

Picture Cards

Use with "Splendid Sort" on page 222.

TEC41049

TEC41049

TEC41049

TEC41049

TEC41049

TEC41049

TEC41049

TEC41049

TEC41049

TEC41049

TEC41049

TEC41049

MATH UNITS

Harvesting Math Ideas

You'll harvest oodles of compliments from your little ones about these fun math ideas!

Number of the Day
Number sense

Post a supersize jack-o'-lantern cutout without a mouth. Place a supply of black paper triangles (teeth), a set of number cards, and a large foam die nearby. Each morning, have a youngster roll the die and count the dots. Then invite him to put that number of teeth on the jack-o'-lantern and post the matching number card beside the jack-o'-lantern. If desired, use a different set of cutouts each month, such as a turkey with feathers in November and an evergreen tree with ornaments in December.

Tracey Morrissey
Good Shepherd Creative Play
Pearl River, NY

Crows in the Field
Reinforcing shapes

To make this adorable project, a child uses a cotton ball to sweep green paint on a sheet of paper to make a field. She dots yellow paint on the field so it resembles corn. Then she glues black construction paper squares and triangles to the paper, as shown, so they resemble crows. She identifies the shapes used for her picture. Then she attaches eye and beak cutouts.

Lisa Drummond, Catholic Charities Diocese of Metuchen
Phillipsburg, NJ

Buying Apples
Number recognition

Label copies of the storefront patterns from page 229 with different numbers and place them in a pocket chart. Then secretly hide an apple cutout behind a storefront. Lead youngsters in reciting the chant below. Then invite a volunteer to name a number and look behind the corresponding storefront to see whether the apple is there. Continue until the apple has been found.

Apple, apple
In a store.
Where are you hiding?
We want more!

LuAnn Ryan, Happiness House, Geneva, NY

Nifty Number Line
Counting, making sets

Divide and label a length of bulletin board paper, as shown, and set a tub of jumbo pom-poms nearby. Read each number and enlist your little ones to help you place that number of pom-poms beneath the numeral. Glue the pom-poms in place to make a permanent number line, or place the paper and pom-poms at a center for independent practice.

Lizzie Vena, Upper Gwynedd Child Learning Center, North Wales, PA

All Kinds of Socks
Sorting

Enlist parents' help in gathering a collection of socks that have lost their mates. Near the socks, set out plastic hoops labeled with sorting guidelines. Encourage youngsters to examine each sock and place it in the correct hoop. Once all the socks have been sorted, invite youngsters to name other ways the socks can be sorted. Change the hoop labels to reflect one of the suggestions, and then sort the socks again.

Nancy M. Lotzer, Farmer's Branch, TX

Stripes

Solids

Fancy Turkeys
Number recognition, counting

To prepare for little ones to make this whimsical Thanksgiving decoration, set out a supply of small baking potatoes, frilled toothpicks, and golf tees. Also provide craft glue and construction paper beaks, wattles, and eyes. Place a list, like the one shown, and a sample turkey near the supplies. Help each child read the list and construct a turkey.

Jennifer Pyle
Westminster School for Young Children
Durham, NC

8
2
2
1
1

No Peeking
Shape identification

Place a supply of craft foam shapes in a bag. Have a volunteer close her eyes and take a shape from the bag. While her eyes are closed, encourage her to feel the shape and then name it. Invite her to open her eyes and check her answer.

Holly Morales, Shining Light Preschool, Pleasanton, CA

Make a Copy
Patterning

For this partner center, place two ice cube trays end to end and set a tub of pom-poms nearby. One child places pom-poms in the top row of the trays to make a pattern. His partner copies the pattern in the remaining row. Invite the youngsters to switch roles and repeat the activity.

Peggy Kenney
Dwire School
Camarillo, CA

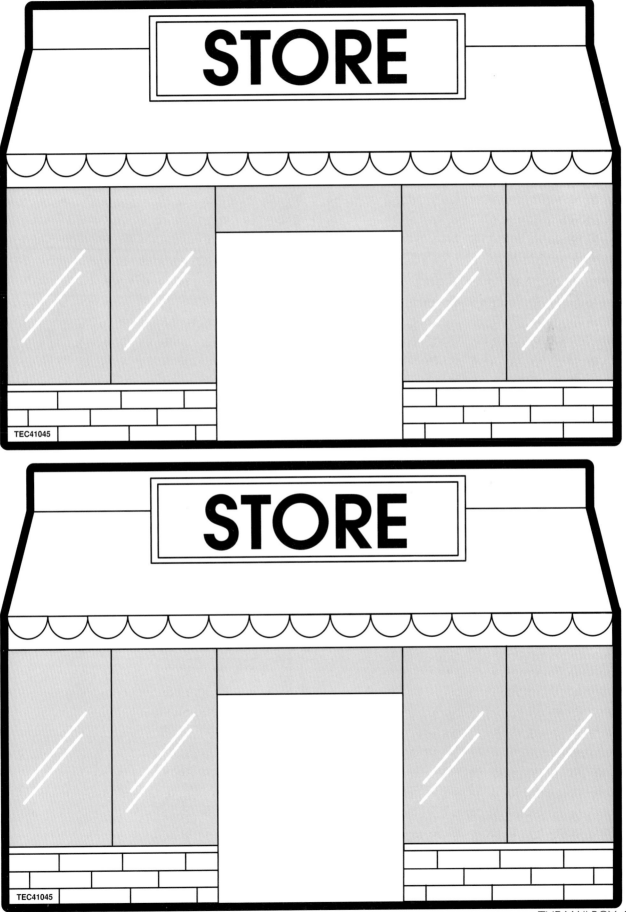

STORE

STORE

TEC41045

TEC41045

Crazy About Numbers

From centers to large-group activities, here's just what you need to stir up a bunch of number-related fun!

Hat Hoopla

One-to-one correspondence, problem solving

Use the patterns on page 233 to prepare an equal number of head and hat cutouts. Display the heads and distribute a few of the hats. Keep the leftover hats out of sight. Invite each child with a hat cutout to put it on a head cutout. Help students decide how many more hats are needed. Then reveal the leftover hats. Ask students to count the hats before inviting volunteers to put one on each head cutout.

Louise Frankel, Family Development Daycare
Plainfield, NJ

Boot Bonanza

Counting pairs

For this flannelboard activity, cut one pair of boots from each of the following felt colors: red, brown, black, blue, yellow. Display the boots. Then lead youngsters through the rhyme. Ask each named student to remove the appropriate pair of boots from the display.

Five pairs of boots
On the classroom floor—
[Child's name] takes the red boots.
Now there are four.

Four pairs of boots—
Count and see.
[Child's name] takes the brown boots.
Now there are three.

Three pairs of boots—
Some old, some new.
[Child's name] takes the black boots.
Now there are two.

Two pairs of boots
For outdoor fun—
[Child's name] takes the blue boots.
Now there is one.

One pair of boots
Still left in the line—
I'll take the yellow pair
Because they are mine!

Marie E. Cecchini, West Dundee, IL

Cuckoo for Cookies

Matching sets to numbers

This center is sure to draw a crowd. Label ten white rectangles (glasses of milk) with numbers 1 to 10. Also cut out ten cookie shapes and draw on them sets of chocolate chips to match the numbers on the glasses. A child counts the chocolate chips on each cookie and then places the cookie with its matching glass.

Michele Rippy
First Baptist Church Parents' Day Out Program
Clarksville, TN

On a Roll!

Counting

To prepare for this partner game, draw two grids with a matching number of spaces. Also provide two sets of craft foam cutouts and a large foam die. A player rolls the die, counts the dots, and puts a matching number of cutouts on her grid. Play continues in turn until all the spaces are filled on one player's board.

Sandy Barker
Early Childhood Family Education
Cottage Grove, MN

Stockings in a Row

Number order

Number each of ten stocking cutouts from 1 to 10. Display the stockings out of sequence in a row. Lead students in reading the row of numbers and guide them to notice that the numbers are not in order. Enlist volunteers to help you rearrange the stockings so they are in the correct order.

Colleen Higgins, Children's Garden, St. Davids, PA

A Nifty Nest
Making sets

At a center, place a nest made from brown paper shreds and a disposable bowl. Also provide number cards programmed with matching sets and enough large yellow pom-poms (chicks) to represent the largest number. A child takes a card, reads the number, and places a matching set of chicks in the nest. He removes the chicks from the nest and plays another round.

Carole Watkins, Crown Point, IN

10, 9, 8...

Blast Off
Counting backward

Get little ones moving with this large-group activity. Have a youngster (astronaut) sit in a chair in an open area. Gather the remaining students in a circle around the chair and have them point their raised arms toward the center of the circle so they resemble the nose cone of a rocket. Lead the group in counting backward from ten. When they reach zero, have them "launch" the astronaut by dropping their arms and standing back. Then invite the astronaut to "fly" about the room.

Beverly Robinson, God's World Preschool and Daycare, Prescott Valley, AZ

Bears in a Cave
Comparing sets

Give each child in a small group a cave cutout and ten bear-shaped crackers. Also give each child a card that shows a number from 1 to 10. Ask each child to read his card and put the matching number of bears on his cave. To guide youngsters to compare their bear sets, ask, "Which cave has the most (fewest) bears?" Continue by collecting the cards and repeating the activity. Then invite little ones to eat their bears.

Leslie Blom
Central Elementary
Bellevue, NE

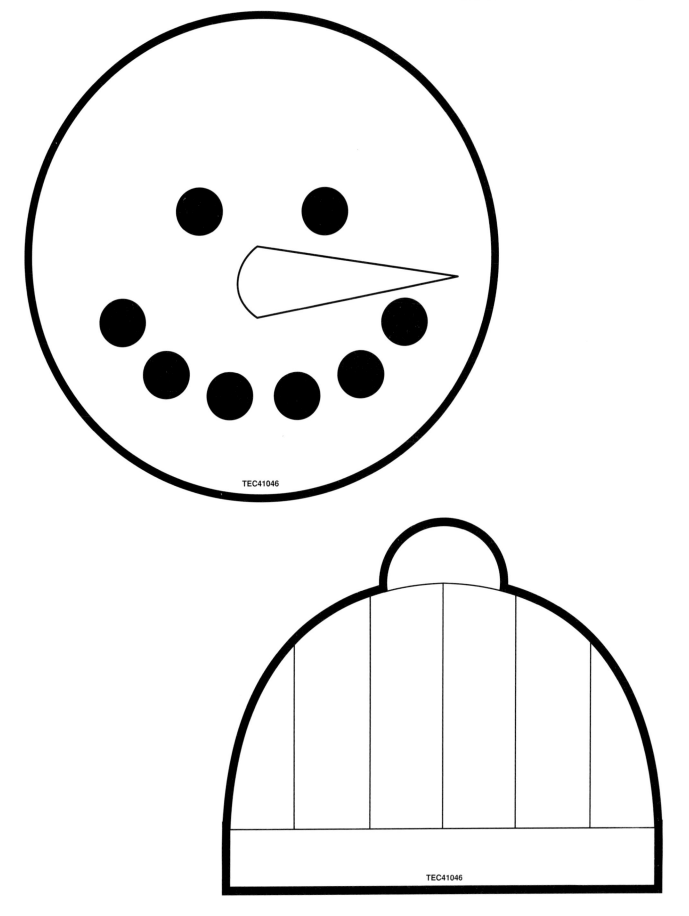

TEC41046

TEC41046

Math With Chicken Little

Read aloud the traditional story of *Chicken Little*. Then guide youngsters through this selection of fine-feathered math activities!

ideas contributed by Elizabeth Cook, St. Louis, MO

The Sky Is Falling!
Counting

Seat a child in the middle of your large-group area. Have him close his eyes. Then drop large brown pom-poms (acorns) on his head as he counts the number of acorns aloud. Encourage him to name the number of acorns that were dropped. Then prompt him to say, "The sky is falling!" Repeat the activity with a different youngster and number of acorns.

Feather Find
Sorting

Gather large and small craft feathers in yellow, white, brown, and red to represent the feathers of Chicken Little, Goosey Loosey, Ducky Lucky, and Cocky Locky. Place feathers around the room. To begin, tell youngsters that Chicken Little and some of his friends have lost several feathers. Have students find the feathers and place them in a pile. Have youngsters help you sort the feathers by color. Then help them re-sort the feathers by size.

Chicken, Goose, Chicken, Goose

Patterning

Cut out several copies of the character cards on page 236. (Remove any characters that aren't in your rendition of the story.) Have students revisit the characters and their names. Then place cards on your floor in a simple pattern. After youngsters read the pattern aloud, help them extend it.

Go to page 237 for a reproducible counting activity filled with learning fun!

Lining Up

Ordinal numbers

Have each child cut out a copy of the character cards on page 236. Revisit the story with your students. Have students remove any characters not in your rendition of the story. Then encourage each youngster to attach the characters in the correct story order to a strip of paper. Ask students questions involving number order and positional words, such as "Who is first in line?" and "Who is behind Goosey Loosey?"

Falling Numbers

Identifying numbers

Attach magnetic numbers to the top of a magnetic board (or cookie sheet). Attach a copy of the chick card (Chicken Little) from page 236 to the bottom of the board. Say, "The [five] is falling! The [five] is falling!" Then encourage a child to remove the number five, make it "fall" on Chicken Little's head, and then leave it at the bottom of the board. Continue in the same way with each remaining number.

Donna Olp, St. Gregory the Great Preschool, South Euclid, OH

Picking Flowers
Counting, recognizing colors

To prepare for this adorable activity, make six colorful flower cutouts (pattern on page 241) and ready them for flannelboard use. (If desired, also attach raindrop and sun cutouts to your board to match the rhyme text.) Then lead youngsters in saying the rhyme. Ask the named student to remove the appropriate flower. Then repeat the rhyme five more times, changing the number to match the flowers on the board.

[Six] little flowers standing in a row.
With sun and water, they will surely grow.
When all the children came out to play,
[Child's name] picked the [color] flower and ran away.

Roberta Jackson
GOCAA Head Start
Ironwood, MI

Check This Out!

To reinforce patterning, Rhonda Urfey of Allen A. Greenleaf School, Waterdown, Ontario, Canada, likes to take on the role of the pattern police. When she sees a youngster making a pattern during center time, she dons a police hat, makes a siren noise, and announces that the pattern police have found a pattern. Then she gives the youngster a ticket with a smiley sticker on it. What a fun way to reinforce math skills!

Shapely Mistakes
Shapes

During this activity, little ones get the chance to teach the teacher! Name a shape but then draw a different shape on the board. Youngsters will quickly point out the mistake you have made. Invite a volunteer to name the shape you have drawn. Assure youngsters that you know which shape to draw now and ask them for one more chance. Then draw the correct shape on the board. Play several rounds of this fun game!

Loreen Forella
Great Beginnings
Pleasantville, NY

This is a square.

Flower Pattern

Use with "Buzzing Around" on page 239 and "Picking Flowers" on page 240.

Bee Pattern

Use with "Buzzing Around" on page 239.

TEC41048

TEC41048

A Math Picnic

Munch on some picnic-themed fun with this collection of marvelous math ideas!

Ants on a Blanket
Number recognition, counting

Give each child in a small group ten pom-poms (ants) and a sheet of construction paper or patterned scrapbooking paper (picnic blanket). Place a stack of number cards facedown. Then lead students in saying the rhyme shown. Invite a little one to take a card and read the number. Direct each youngster to place a matching number of ants on his blanket. After checking his work, have him remove the ants from the blanket to get ready for another round.

Ants on a blanket,
One, two, three.
Ants on a blanket;
How many can there be?

Tammy Kennington
Calvary Preschool
Colorado Springs, CO

7

Yummy Favorites
Organizing data

Youngsters share their preferred picnic entrees with this simple idea! In advance, attach to your wall a simple picnic basket cutout labeled with the headings shown. Have each child color a copy of the food card from page 245 that matches her picnic preference. Help her write her name on her card and then attach it to the cutout under the appropriate heading. Lead youngsters in counting the hamburgers and hot dogs and comparing the numbers.

Lucia Kemp Henry, Fallon, NV

hamburger   hot dog

Karla   Rebecca   Ginny   Anthony   Alfonso

Richie

Red, White, Red, White
Patterning

Draw a grid on a square piece of red bulletin board paper. Then laminate the grid and place it in a center. Provide a container of white construction paper squares that match the size of the squares on the grid. A youngster places white squares on every other grid square to make a lovely patterned picnic blanket!

Keely Saunders, Bonney Lake Early Childhood Education and Assistance Program, Bonney Lake, WA

Getting Ready
Making sets

To prepare for this center activity, stock a picnic basket with disposable plates, cups, napkins, and cutlery for eight place settings. Place a picnic blanket nearby. A child spreads out the picnic blanket. Then she arranges the items from the basket to make eight place settings around the edges of the blanket.

Marie E. Cecchini
West Dundee, IL

Picnic Guests
Nonstandard measurement

Guess who's coming to this picnic. Ants! Place a supply of ant cutouts (patterns on page 245) near a table. Invite a group of youngsters to join you at the table for an imaginary picnic. To begin, show the group one of the ants. Ask each child to predict how many ants he thinks it will take to form a line that runs the length of the table. Place the ant on the table to start the line. Then enlist students' help in adding ants to the line. Continue until the line runs the length of the table. Lead youngsters in counting the ants and comparing the number to their predictions.

Which Blanket?

Sorting by size

Enlarge and reduce the ant cards on page 245 to make a supply of ants in different sizes. Cut out three fabric rectangles in different sizes and label each one with a heading and a corresponding ant card. Place the remaining ants in a small bag and set the bag nearby. In turn, invite a youngster to take an ant from the bag. Have her compare it to the ant on each blanket label and then place it on the matching blanket.

Shonda Yates
University of Kentucky Mommy and Me
Lexington, KY

Hot off the Grill

One-to-one correspondence

Use this center activity to serve up a helping of fine-motor skills along with some math practice. On a plastic serving tray, place an unequal number of tagboard hamburger and hot dog cards (see page 245). Provide a plate for each card. Also provide a pair of tongs. A child arranges the plates on a work surface. Then she uses the tongs to pick up each card and place it on a separate plate. She counts the hot dogs and hamburgers and compares the numbers using words such as *more* and *less.*

Lucia Kemp Henry
Fallon, NV

Wonderful Watermelon

Matching numbers to sets

To make watermelon slices, cut several pink paper plates in half. Use permanent markers to draw the rind and a different number of seeds on each plate. Place the slices in a row on a work surface and provide number cards to match the numbers of seeds. A youngster counts the seeds on each slice and then places the matching number card above the slice. **For an added challenge,** he arranges the slices in correct number order.

Lucia Kemp Henry

Hamburger and Hot Dog Cards
Use with "Yummy Favorites" on page 242 and "Hot off the Grill" on page 244.

TEC41049

TEC41049

Ant Patterns
Use with "Picnic Guests" on page 243 and "Which Blanket?" on page 244.

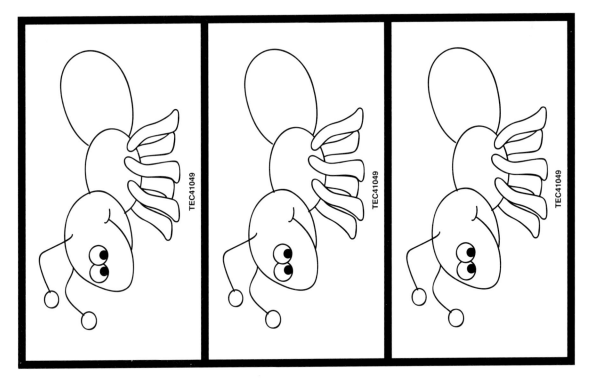

TEC41049

TEC41049

TEC41049

Let's Learn About Colors!

Find and Place

Youngsters will be tickled pink with this fun center-time color search! Attach a length of bulletin board paper to a table. During center time, encourage youngsters to find objects in the room that are the same color as the paper. Then encourage students to place the items on the paper. At the end of the day, have little ones look over the objects and confirm that they are the correct color. Then prompt youngsters to put the objects away.

Cindy Laskowsky
New Adventures Child Development Center
Prescott, AZ

Colorful Fingers

Obtain inexpensive white gloves and then paint each finger one of five different colors. Gather a small group of youngsters and help each child put on a glove. Don't forget to wear a glove yourself. Have students hold up their red fingers. Then lead them in singing the song shown. Repeat the song for each remaining finger, changing the underlined word to reflect the appropriate color.

(sung to the tune of "Where Is Thumbkin?")

Where is [red man]? Where is [red man]?
Here he is! Here he is!
What a lovely color. What a lovely color.
Goodbye, [red]. Goodbye, [red].

Keep fingers in a fist.
Hold up the red finger.
Shake hand from side to side.
Form a fist again.

Jane Mandia, Little Friends Preschool, Marlboro, NY

Color Booklets

For each child, accordion-fold a length of paper to make four sections. Label the top section with a color word. Then have each child add items of the corresponding color to each section, such as pieces of paint cards to the second section, magazine pictures to the third section, and paint splotches to the final section. If desired, have youngsters make a color booklet for each primary and secondary color.

Tracey Mikos
Sacred Heart School
New Smyrna Beach, FL

Simple Secondary Colors

This easy project will seem magical to your little ones! Help a youngster press a hand in a shallow pan of red paint and then make a print on a sheet of paper. Help her keep the red hand out of the way while she repeats the process with her remaining hand and blue paint. Finally, have her rub her hands together and say, "Abracadabra." Then prompt her to make a purple handprint on the page. If desired, have students repeat the activity with different colors to create orange and green handprints.

Noel James
Greater Wenatchee Parent-Child Preschool
Wenatchee, WA

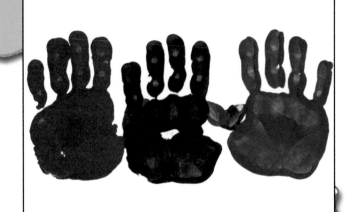

That's My Color!

Read aloud a simple book about colors, such as *I Went Walking* by Sue Williams or *Warthogs Paint: A Messy Color Book* by Pamela Duncan Edwards. Then give each child a square of construction paper that matches one of the colors in the book. Reread the story, prompting students to hold their papers in the air whenever their color is mentioned.

Barbara Mahanovich
Gibbs Family Daycare
Hermitage, PA

Tap and Sing

Mount colorful pieces of construction paper to your wall in the order shown. Then lead students in singing the song as you touch each piece of paper to reflect the lyrics. When youngsters are comfortable with the song, invite a volunteer to take on your role.

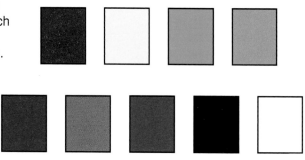

(sung to the tune of "Head and Shoulders")

Red and yellow, blue and green, blue and green.
Red and yellow, blue and green, blue and green.
Brown, orange, purple, black, and white.
Red and yellow, blue and green, blue and green.

Amber Dingman, Play 'N' Learn Family Child Care, Sterling, MI

Dark and Light

Ask permission to gather several paint sample cards from a home improvement store. Place the cards in a bag. Then make a chart similar to the one shown. Have a child choose a card. Read aloud the name of the paint color. Ask students why they think the color has that name. Then have them decide whether the particular color is light or dark and encourage a child to attach the card to the chart. Continue with each remaining card.

Shelley Hoster, Jack & Jill Early Learning Center, Norcross, GA

Hand Pointers

Attach colorful hand cutouts to separate paint stir sticks to make pointers. During center time, encourage a child to choose a pointer and name the color. Prompt him to hunt for items in the classroom that are the same color and then tap them with his pointer. Have him repeat the activity with other pointers.

Darla Rogers
Miami Valley Child Development Centers, Inc.
Dayton, OH

Little Mouse, Little Mouse

Place several different-colored construction paper houses on the floor in your circle-time area. While youngsters cover their eyes, place a mouse cutout under one of the houses. Instruct them to uncover their eyes; then have a child name a house color. Lead students in chanting, "Little mouse, little mouse, are you in the [color name] house?" Have a child lift the appropriate house. If the mouse is not there, have students continue guessing and chanting. If the mouse is revealed, play another round of the game.

Christina Lembo, Tender Garden, Levittown, NY

Back to the Box

Place a different-colored sheet of construction paper in each corner of your room. Have students stand in the middle of the room (crayon box). Say, "Crayon color mix-up!" Then close your eyes and count to ten. As you count, each youngster tiptoes toward a corner. When you reach ten, call out a color and then open your eyes. Students in the corresponding corner go back to the crayon box until the end of the game. Repeat the process until only a few students remain out of the crayon box. Then have everyone join in for another round!

Sanine Beck, Little Learners Preschool and Academy, Lincoln, NE

Little Painter

This activity is an excellent color assessment! Cut out colorful copies of the paint can on page 250. Give a paintbrush to a child and ask him to find the color red. When he locates the red paint can, he brushes it with his paintbrush. Continue with each remaining color.

Karen Eiben, The Learning House Preschool, LaSalle, IL

Paint Can Pattern
Use with "Little Painter" on page 249.

Paint

TEC41044

THEMATIC UNITS

Start Your Engines: It's Time for Preschool!

Let's Go for a Drive!
School tour

To help little ones get to know their classroom and school, take them on this adorable "driving" tour! Make several red stop signs and attach each one to a place of interest, such as the block center, restroom, gym, office, and library. Give each youngster a paper plate (steering wheel) and encourage her to pretend to start her engine and test her horn. Then lead your line of cars to each stop sign, pausing to introduce the different locations of interest and the people you meet along the way!

Nancy Reed, Woodland Early Learning Center, Carpentersville, IL

Vroom, Vroom, Vroom!
Circle-time activity

Youngsters are sure to request this color identification activity again and again! Enlarge the car pattern on page 256 and make several colorful copies. Then lightly tape the cars to your board. Help little ones identify the colors of the cars. Then prompt them to cover their eyes and say, "Vroom, vroom, vroom!" Remove a car and have students uncover their eyes. Then help youngsters identify the color of the car that "drove away." Play several rounds of this fun game.

Melissa Letson, Metrowest Early Childhood Center
Framingham, MA

Fill 'er Up!
Job display

To make this cute job display, enlarge the fuel pump pattern on page 256 and then make several copies. Cut out the pumps and label them with different job titles. Then enlarge the car pattern on page 256 and make a class supply of copies. Label each car with a different student's name. Display the pumps as shown. Then attach a car near each pump. If desired, embellish the display with checkered flags.

Brooke Beverly, Dudley Elementary, Dudley, MA

Line Leader

Caboose

Joshua

Misty

Lights

Plant Care

Brianna

Lee

For simple cubby tags and nametags, personalize colorful copies of the car and fuel pump patterns on page 256. Then cut them out and laminate them for durability.

Rattletrap Car

Phyllis Root

illustrated by Jill Barton

A Broken-Down Car
Responding to a book through art

To begin, read aloud *Rattletrap Car* by Phyllis Root. Junie, Jakie, Poppa, and the baby want to go to the lake, but will their rattletrap car make it? Not without a variety of props and the sticky properties of chocolate marshmallow fudge delight! After the read-aloud, give each child an enlarged copy of the car pattern on page 256. Provide a variety of craft materials and a container of brown paint mixed with white glue (chocolate marshmallow fudge delight). A youngster uses a paintbrush to apply the sticky dessert to her car. Then she places a variety of colorful items in the mixture. Why, this chocolate marshmallow fudge delight is just as sticky as that in the book!

Driving to Preschool
Song
Encourage each child to "steer" a paper plate steering wheel while you lead the class in singing this song!

(sung to the tune of "I've Been Working on the Railroad")

I am driving to my preschool
All the livelong day.
I am driving to my preschool
So I can learn and play.
Can't you hear the engine roaring?
I've got to go fast, you see;
I can hear my teacher calling,
"Come and learn with me!"

Won't you ride with me? Won't you ride with me?
Won't you ride to school with me?
Won't you ride with me? Won't you ride with me?
Won't you ride to school with me?

Shelley Hoster, Jack and Jill Early Learning Center, Norcross, GA

Check This Out!
Suzanne Foote of East Ithaca Preschool, Ithaca, New York, combines her art and water table centers for her car-themed unit! She has youngsters move cars through a shallow pan of paint and then onto a sheet of paper. Then she prompts students to take the cars to the car wash (a tub of water set up with washcloths and sponges). Now those cars are squeaky clean!

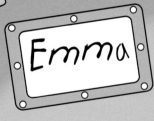

Vroom, vroom, vroom! It's [Ashley] at the wheel
Of [her] super-duper shiny new automobile!
[She] says, "I'm late, so I can't move slow!
"I'll see you later. Time to go, go, go!"

Who's at the Wheel?
Getting acquainted
Make simple license plate name cards like the ones shown. Then gather youngsters and show them a card. Help students identify the name and corresponding classmate. Then lead them in reciting the rhyme shown, inserting the appropriate name. Prompt the child whose name is on the card to zoom around the circle and then settle back in her spot before you show students the next name card. What fun!

Let's Race!
Display

Have each child pose holding a pot lid so it resembles a steering wheel; then take his photo. Encourage him to use shape cutouts to make a simple racecar as shown. Then help him write his first initial on his car and attach his trimmed photo. Display the cars along with crafty black-and-white flags and the title "Racing to Preschool!"

Nanette Sposito, Little Wonders Preschool, Oakley, CA

Where Are the Wheels?
Snack

Give each child a copy of page 257 and a bag of circular mini crackers or cookies. Prompt each child to identify the shape of the treats. Then have him put two wheels on each car. Finally, encourage him to nibble on this "wheel-y" tasty treat!

Tunnels and Bridges
Sand table

Here's an idea that's sure to get youngsters thinking about positional words! Partially bury small cardboard tubes (tunnels) in your sand table so that the openings show. Also place wooden blocks between mounds of sand to make bridges. Provide a variety of small toy cars. No doubt youngsters will love pushing the cars through the tunnels and over the bridges.

Erica Haver, Herkimer BOCES, Herkimer, NY

Car Pattern

Use with "Vroom, Vroom, Vroom!" on page 252, "Fill 'er Up!" and "A Broken-Down Car" on page 253, and for cubby tags and nametags.

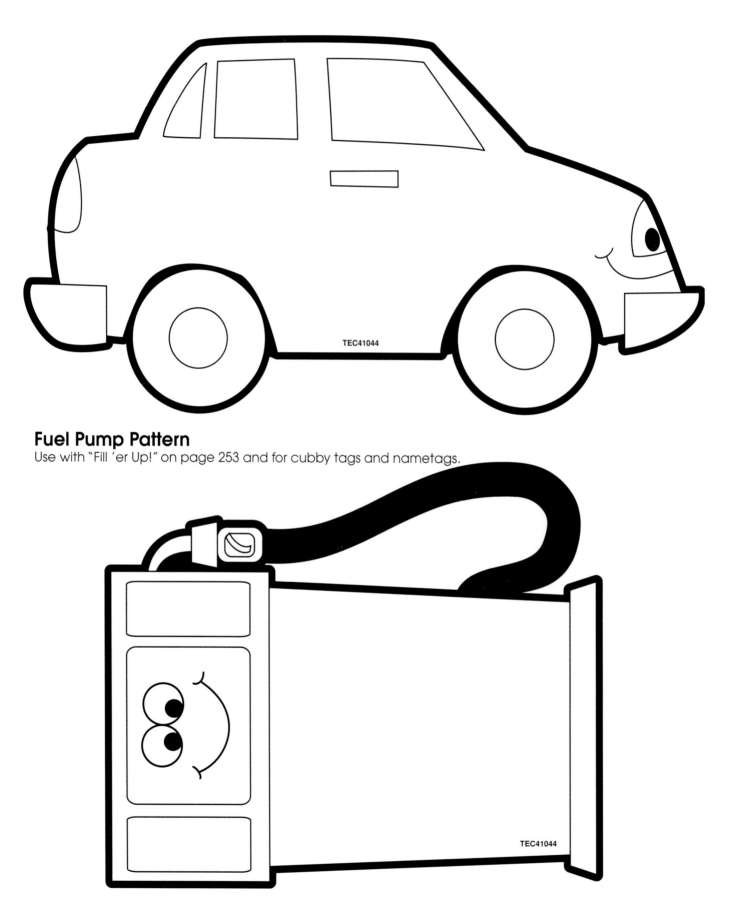

TEC41044

Fuel Pump Pattern

Use with "Fill 'er Up!" on page 253 and for cubby tags and nametags.

TEC41044

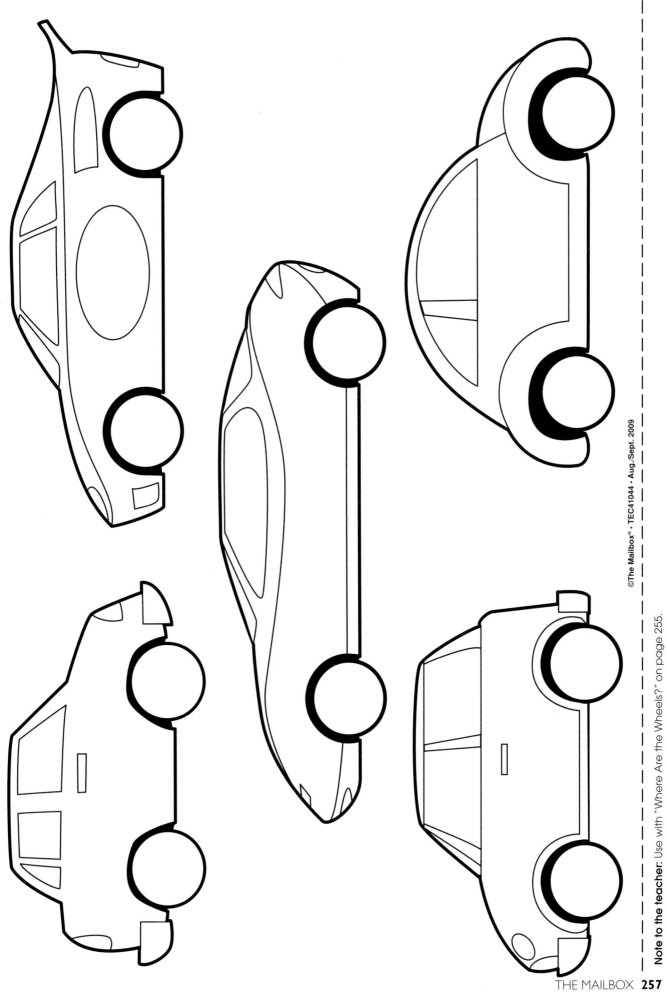

Note to the teacher: Use with "Where Are the Wheels?" on page 255.

Pleasing Pie

P Is for Pie
Beginning sound /p/

This pie is filled with a variety of unique items—all beginning with /p/! Cut out a copy of the cards on page 262. Then place the cards facedown around an empty aluminum pie tin. Have a child choose a card and say the name of the picture. Help him understand that the picture's name begins with /p/. Then have him put the card in the tin. When the tin is full of cards, have youngsters shake pretend spices over the pie. Then have them help place a circle of play dough over the tin and crimp the edges so it resembles a real pie!

Mary Robles
Little Acorns Preschool
Milwaukie, OR

Fabulous Fillings!
Organizing data, sorting

Draw two circles (pies) on a length of bulletin board paper and label them "Cherry" and "Blueberry." Collect a can of cherry pie filling and a can of blueberry pie filling. Allow each child to taste the fillings. Then have him choose a colored construction paper square to represent his favorite filling. Help each child glue his square to the appropriate pie. Then lead youngsters in counting and comparing the sets of squares.

Cherry   Blueberry

Add Some Fruit!
Developing fine-motor skills

Place fruit cutouts in a tub. Place a large pie cutout and a pair of scissors nearby. A youngster chooses a piece of fruit and cuts it into small pieces. Then he glues the pieces to the pie. When the pie is covered with pieces of fruit, attach brown construction paper strips, if desired. Then display the pie in your classroom.

Parachute Pie
Developing gross-motor skills

Have youngsters stand around a parachute and hold the parachute's edge. Tell students to pretend that the parachute is a piecrust. Then encourage them to raise the crust as you call out several students' names. Prompt the called students (pie filling) to run under the crust and sit on the floor beneath it as the remaining youngsters pull the edges of the crust downward. Repeat the activity several times, calling on different youngsters.

Colleen Dabney, Williamsburg, VA

Flies in Pie
Expressing oneself through art

In advance, mix food coloring into corn syrup to create a brownish-yellow color. Read aloud the hilarious story *Thelonius Monster's Sky-High Fly Pie* by Judy Sierra. Then prompt youngsters to make their own fly pie! Encourage each child to brush the tinted syrup over a brown tagboard pie cutout (pattern on page 263) so it resembles the goo and crust from the story. Then have her sprinkle black hole-punched dots (flies) over the goo. If desired, encourage her to top the pie with strips of brown rickrack. Allow the project to dry for several days.

adapted from an idea by Tina Borek
Gateway Christian School, Roswell, NM

THELONIUS MONSTER'S SKY-HIGH FLY PIE

A revolting rhyme
by Judy Sierra
with delicious drawings
by Edward Koren

Piecrust Treat
Following directions
Purchase refrigerated piecrust dough and give each child a small portion. Have her manipulate the dough as desired. Then encourage her to flatten the dough and place it on a cookie sheet. Have students sprinkle cinnamon and sugar over the dough. Then bake the dough at the temperature indicated on the package until it's golden brown. When the snack is cool, encourage each youngster to nibble on her treat.

Marie E. Cecchini
West Dundee, IL

Pie Wishes
Participating in a song
Lead youngsters in singing this adorable little song about pie! Repeat the song several times, having youngsters suggest a different filling each time.

*(sung to the tune of
"If You're Happy and You Know It")*

Oh, I wish I were a little piece of pie. Yum! Yum!
Oh, I wish I were a little piece of pie. Yum! Yum!
Filled with [apples] all around
With a crust so warm and brown—
Oh, I wish I were a little piece of pie. Yum! Yum!

adapted from an idea by Bill Freiermuth
Cromwell-Wright Elementary, Cromwell, MN

Check This Out!
For a fun pie-related dramatic-play center, Diana Parton of West Plains Elementary, West Plains, Missouri, provides a variety of fun props! She adds aluminum pie tins, craft foam crust cutouts, and empty spice containers to the center. She also provides sponges cut into cubes for a fun pie filling!

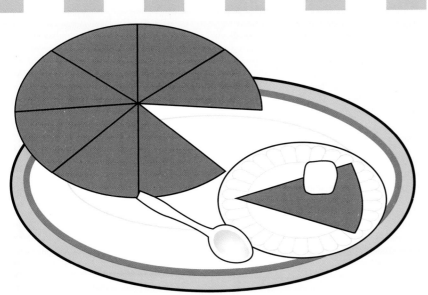

How Many Spoons?
Counting

Divide a circle cutout into several wedges so it resembles a pie. Then cut apart the wedges. Collect a supply of plastic spoons, paper plates, and cotton balls (whipped cream). Rearrange the pie wedges to form a circle. Have youngsters help you count the pieces of pie. Encourage students to decide how many plates are needed to serve all the pieces and then put each piece on a plate. Repeat the process with spoons and whipped cream.

adapted from an idea by Margaret Hamilton
Lakeside Pre-K, Rossville, GA

Twister Game Time
Identifying colors

Place a Twister game mat on the floor of your classroom. Explain that the circles on the mat represent pies. Then point to each color of pie and assign it a pie flavor (*cherry, lemon, blueberry, and lime*). Call on a child and then announce a type of pie. Have the child stand on the appropriate circle and name the color of the pie. Repeat the process until the mat is filled with preschoolers. Then clear the mat and begin another round!

Colleen Dabney, Williamsburg, VA

Roll, Add, Bake, Done
Participating in a song or rhyme
This catchy yet simple little song is sure to be a favorite!

*(sung to the tune of
"Row, Row, Row Your Boat")*

Roll, roll, roll the dough.
Making pie is fun!
Add the fruit and bake it up.
Now the pie is done.

Marie E. Cecchini
West Dundee, IL

Beginning Sound Cards

Use with "*P* Is for Pie" on page 258.

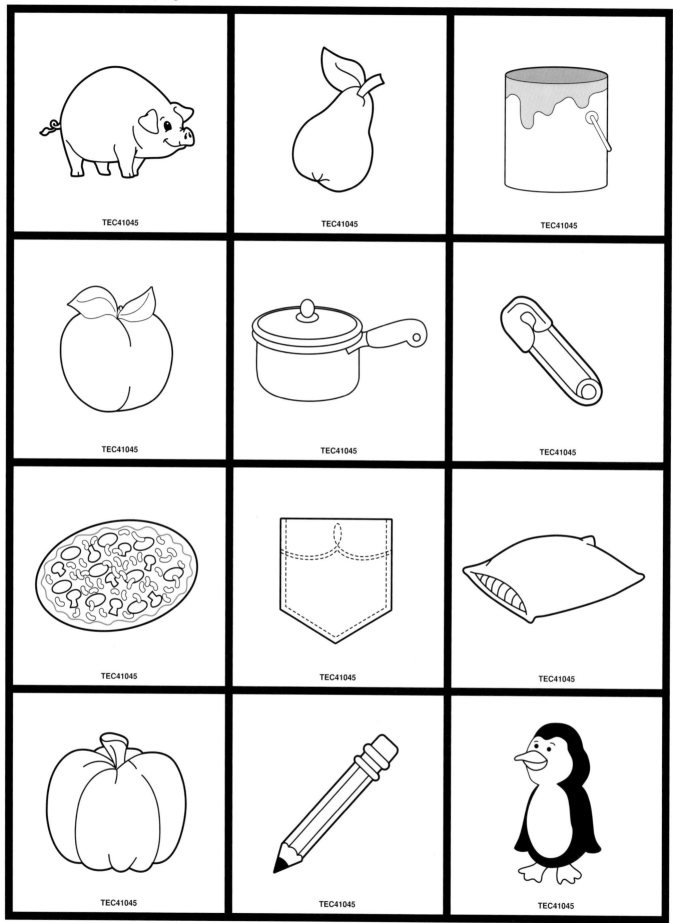

TEC41045

TEC41045

TEC41045

TEC41045

TEC41045

TEC41045

TEC41045

TEC41045

TEC41045

TEC41045

TEC41045

TEC41045

TEC41045

My Body

Eyes and Hair

Little ones identify their hair and eye color with this simple idea! Give each child a sheet of construction paper labeled with a circle and an eye shape. Encourage him to draw a face on the circle. Then have him choose paper shreds that match his hair color and glue them to the circle. Next, encourage him to choose a crayon that matches his eye color and color the eye. Have him brush glue over the eye and sprinkle glitter over the glue to give the eye a little sparkle. Finally, write the youngster's hair and eye color on the paper.

Samantha Hendricks, Hand in Hand Academy, Lutz, FL

Sammy

Hair: brown   Eyes: green

My Doctor Bag

Help youngsters understand that doctors help keep bodies healthy! Make a simple construction paper doctor's bag, as shown, and gather a variety of health-related props, such as cotton swabs, adhesive bandages, cotton balls, and tongue depressors. Read aloud a story about doctors. Then ask youngsters to share information they know or learned about doctors. Each time a child shares information, prompt her to choose an item and attach it to the doctor's bag. Continue until the doctor's bag is full of items.

Karen Cox and David Cox, The Edwards-Wilson Center, Chesapeake, VA

Let's Get Clean!

Ask youngsters why we take baths and showers, leading them to conclude that being clean will help our bodies stay healthy. Next, have each child place a dot of glue on a paper plate. Then prompt her to place the end of a length of blue yarn in the glue. Encourage her to repeat the process several times. When the glue is dry, suspend the resulting showerheads from your ceiling as a reminder to youngsters that it's important to keep their bodies clean.

Keely Peasner, Liberty Ridge Head Start, Bonney, WA

Body Part Sort

Place hand and foot cutouts in your pocket chart as shown. Then cut out a copy of the cards on page 266 and place them in a gift bag. Prompt a child to choose a card and describe the action shown. Then have him place the card beneath the main body part used in the action. Continue with each remaining card.

Kathryn Davenport, Partin Elementary, Oviedo, FL

Body Snackers

To make this simple snack, a child spreads flavored cream cheese or frosting over a section of graham cracker. Then she adds a mini sandwich cookie head and pretzel stick arms and legs. What a tasty treat!

Jeanette Anderson, Jeanette's Tots, Otsego, MN

Hand and Foot Action Cards
Use with "Body Part Sort" on page 265.

©The Mailbox® • TEC41045 • Oct./Nov. 2009

Note to the teacher: Give each child a copy of this page. Name a body part. Then have each child make a mark with a bingo dauber on the pattern's corresponding body part. Continue in the same way.

THE MAILBOX **267**

Penguins

Youngsters will be charmed by this selection of activities about everyone's favorite flightless bird!

Birdie Booklet
Tracking print

This sweet little booklet gives youngsters information about penguins! Make a copy of pages 271 and 272 for each child. Read aloud the pages and have him follow the words with his finger. Have him color his pages as desired. Then encourage him to brush glue over the pictures of ice and snow and sprinkle glitter over the glue. When the glue is dry, help him cut out and assemble the pages beneath a cover labeled "Pleasing Penguins."

Penguins slide. Penguins waddle. 1

Penguins eat. Penguins huddle. 2

Penguins swim, wild and free 3

In the chilly, icy sea. 4

Protect the Egg
Gross-motor skills: balancing

Have students pretend to be emperor penguins. Give each child a beanbag (egg) and encourage her to balance it on her feet, similar to what a real emperor penguin would do. Have students determine different ways they can move while still keeping the egg safe. Encourage them to attempt walking, waddling, jumping, flapping their wings (arms), and hopping—all while balancing the egg.

Donna Ross
Apple Place Nursery School
Chambersburg, PA

Potato Penguins
Developing fine-motor skills

To prepare for this adorable project, slice a large potato in half lengthwise and a smaller potato in half widthwise. Have a child make a black paint print on a sheet of paper using the large potato. Then encourage him to make a white paint print over the black print using the smaller potato. Prompt him to add construction paper details to the resulting penguin. When the paint is dry, cut out the penguins and display them on a wall with aluminum foil icebergs.

Stacy Baker, Early Childhood Center, Hudson, OH

Hungry Babies
Counting, presubtraction skills

Your hungry little penguins will love these word problems and this simple snack! Give each child a cup of fish-shaped crackers and a napkin. Explain that baby penguins are very hungry, and they like to eat fish. Say, "One day, four little fish went swimming." Prompt students to place four fish on their napkins. Tell youngsters that a baby penguin ate two of the fish, and encourage them to eat two crackers. Then ask students how many fish are left. After they respond, repeat the process with another word problem.

Lisa Igou, Silbernagel Elementary, Dickinson, TX

Pip's Nest
Retelling a story

In advance, place small round sponges next to shallow pans of paint in several shades of brown. Read aloud *Where Is Home, Little Pip?* by Karma Wilson, a story in which Pip the penguin leaves her rocky nest and gets lost while chasing a feather. Then have each child make sponge prints on a sheet of construction paper so it resembles Pip's nest. Prompt her to color and cut out a copy of the penguin on page 273 and glue it to the nest. Then encourage her to glue a black feather to the project. Have her tell about Pip, her nest, and the significance of the feather. Then prompt her to share other story details.

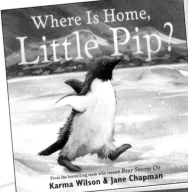

It's Me!
Participating in a group game

"It's me!"

Explain to little ones that mommy penguins go swimming to find food. When they are finished, they come back and find the daddy penguins by listening for their voices. Have one child pretend to be a mommy penguin and go "fishing" in the hall with a classroom helper. Choose a daddy penguin and have him hide from view. Then invite the mommy to come back from her fishing trip. Encourage the daddy to say, "It's me!" Then help the mommy penguin identify the daddy by name.

Maureen Mcinnis, Castle Hill Academy, Medfield, MA

I'm a Little Penguin
Participating in an action song
Lead students in performing this sweet little action song!

(sung to the tune of "I'm a Little Teapot")

I'm a little penguin,
Black and white.
With big orange feet
I'm quite a sight.
I like to play outside
In the ice and snow
'Cause I like the cold,
Don't you know!

Jennifer Wilson, Wonder Years Child Care, Jersey Shore, PA

On the Iceberg
Estimation

Place a bedsheet on your floor. If desired, scatter fish cutouts around the sheet. Tell students that the sheet is an iceberg and they are penguins. Ask them if they believe the whole class will fit on the iceberg. Listen to their responses and then prompt students to stand on the iceberg and evaluate their predictions. Next, have students sit back down; then fold the iceberg in half. Ask students how many classmates will fit on the iceberg. Lead students in counting aloud as you guide them to stand on the iceberg, stopping when it is full of students. Once again, have youngsters evaluate their predictions. Repeat the process several times, folding the sheet in half each time.

Laura Kessler, Stoneridge Elementary, Roseville, CA

Penguins slide. Penguins waddle.

1

Penguins eat. Penguins huddle.

2

Penguins swim, wild and free

3

In the chilly, icy sea.

4

TEC41046

Ice Is Nice!

Here's a slick selection of ice-themed activities just perfect for this chilly season!

Who's on the Iceberg?
Participating in a group game

This shivery game is sure to be a hit with your little ones! Place ice in a resealable plastic bag and secure the sealed bag with tape. Have youngsters sit in a circle. Place an iceberg cutout in the center of the circle. Play a recording of upbeat music and have youngsters pass the bag around the circle. Then stop the music and prompt the child with the bag to sit on the iceberg and pretend to shiver. Play several rounds of this simple game!

Nifty Icicles!
Developing fine-motor skills

This cool craft is surprisingly easy to make! Dip a square of cheesecloth in a pan of diluted glue and then drape the cloth over a foam cone. Sprinkle white or silver glitter over the cloth. When it is dry, remove the resulting icicle from the cone. String several icicles together and suspend them near a window. They look lovely!

Kristina Wisner, Leaping Learners Child Development Center, Hampstead, MD

See page 277 for a nifty project idea with an ice-skating theme!

Iceberg Float
Observing, predicting

Freeze water in containers of different sizes and shapes. Then remove the resulting icebergs and float them in your water table. Place strainers, slotted spoons, and other utensils near the table. Encourage youngsters to predict what will happen to the icebergs throughout the day. Then prompt them to use the utensils to explore the icebergs.

Roxanne LaBell Dearman, Western NC Early Intervention Program for Children Who Are Deaf or Hard of Hearing, Charlotte, NC

A Peachy Igloo!
Following directions

The fruity snack is simple and healthy! To prepare, slice a banana into thick chunks and then cut each chunk in half. To begin, help each child place a peach half on a plate, cut side down. Have her place a banana chunk next to the peach as shown. Then encourage her to spread light whipped topping over the fruit to finish the igloo.

Kathryn Davenport, Partin Elementary, Oviedo, FL

Ice, Nice, Mice
Identifying rhyming words

This rhyming game is prop-free! Name a word from the word list shown. If the word rhymes with *ice,* prompt youngsters to shiver. If the word does not rhyme with *ice,* have them remain still. Continue with the remaining words.

Word list:
nice, shoe, rice, mice, stop, twice, cake, spice, price, shell, vise, dog, lice

Roxanne LaBell Dearman

Icy Stack

Developing spatial skills

Encourage parents to send empty shoeboxes to school so there is one for each student. Tape the shoeboxes closed. Then have each child paint her box white so it resembles a block of ice. When the paint is dry, place the boxes in your block center. Encourage youngsters to use the boxes to build fantastic ice structures.

Beth Klenczar, Flat Rock Community Schools, Flat Rock, MI

A Slippery Song

Participating in an action song

Students will work all of their wiggles out when they perform this cute little song about ice-skating!

(sung to the tune of "Have You Ever Seen a Lassie?")

Have you ever gone ice-skating,   *Pretend to glide about the room.*
Ice-skating, ice-skating?
Have you ever gone ice-skating?
Then whoops—you fell down!   *Fall to the floor.*
One minute, you're standing;   *Stand up.*
The next, you are landing.   *Fall to the floor.*
Have you ever gone ice-skating   *Stand up.*
Then whoops—you fell down!   *Fall to the floor.*

Fresh Food

Counting

What is ice used for? Why, to keep food fresh! Collect a supply of white bottle caps (ice cubes). Place pieces of play food in a cooler. Then place the cooler at a center along with the ice cubes and a die. Two youngsters visit the center. One child rolls the die, counts that number of ice cubes, and places them in the cooler. His partner repeats the process. Youngsters continue taking turns until the cooler is filled with ice. Now that food will stay fresh for a holiday dinner!

adapted from an idea by Becky Crutsinger, Weatherford Christian School, Weatherford, TX

Have each child tear strips of aluminum foil and attach them to a sheet of paper to make an ice-skating rink. Help her color and cut out a copy of the patterns and then glue them to the rink.

Clouds

Your youngsters are sure to love cloudy days with this selection of splendid cloud-themed activities!

Look Up!
Investigating weather

Here's an activity that will help youngsters notice different types of clouds. Give each student a copy of page 282. Have students point to each type of cloud on their sheets and encourage them to describe the clouds. Then have them color the page. Next, have little ones take their pages outside and look at the clouds in the sky. Prompt them to discuss whether any clouds they see look like the ones on the sheet. If desired, take youngsters outside several times to observe the clouds.

Dawn Smith, Dawn's Family Daycare, Wrentham, MA

Below the Clouds
Identifying numbers

Color and cut out a copy of the patterns on page 283. Scatter the pictures on your floor and then place a numbered cloud cutout over each pattern. Scatter extra numbered cloud cutouts as well. Ask, "Where is the helicopter?" Have a child name the number of the cloud he thinks is concealing the helicopter. Then prompt him to lift the cloud. If the helicopter is revealed, he removes the cloud and helicopter and places them nearby. If not, a different child guesses. Continue in the same way with each remaining picture.

Marie E. Cecchini, West Dundee, IL

5

3

8

10

2

Small, Medium, Large
Sorting
Obtain white pom-poms in three different sizes and place them in a container. Put the container at a center along with tweezers and three sheets of blue paper (sky) or sky-themed scrapbooking paper. Encourage a child to use the tweezers to sort the pom-poms onto the pieces of paper.

Amy Durrwachter, Kirkwood Early Childhood Center, Kirkwood, MO, and Clarissa Dwyer, Discovery Kids Preschool, Maple Plain, MN

A Fluffy Snack
Following directions
Place an equal amount of marshmallow fluff and whipped cream cheese in a bowl. Have youngsters help you mix the two items together so they resemble a cloud. Have each child spoon a small amount of the substance onto a blue paper plate (sky). A youngster dips fruit pieces into his cloud and then eats them. Yum!

Rexann Roussel, Narrow Acres Preschool, Paulina, LA

Spilt Milk Clouds
Responding to a story through art
Read aloud the story *It Looked Like Spilt Milk* by Charles G. Shaw. Then give each child a cup with slightly diluted white paint. Encourage her to spill her paint onto a sheet of blue construction paper. Then prompt her to tilt and shake the paper to move the paint. Finally, prompt her to look at the paint spill and name what she believes the spill resembles. Write her words on the paper, as shown.

Alyssa Fisher, Little Beavers Preschool, Corry, PA

My cloud looks like a bunny.

It Looked
Like Spilt Milk

by Charles G. Shaw

Oodles of Raindrops!

Matching uppercase and lowercase letters

Label pairs of raindrops with matching uppercase and lowercase letters. Wrap a lidded box in white paper so it resembles a cloud and cut an opening in the top. If desired, attach pieces of cotton batting to the cloud. Place the cloud on your lap and put the uppercase raindrops nearby. Give each youngster a lowercase raindrop. Tell students that the cloud needs many raindrops. Hold up an uppercase raindrop and have students identify the letter. Then prompt the child with the matching lowercase letter to place both raindrops in the cloud.

Rexann Roussel, Narrow Acres Preschool, Paulina, LA

Cloudy Chorus

Participating in a rhyming song

Lead youngsters in singing this song several times while they drift about the room like clouds on a breezy day.

(sung to the tune of "Twinkle, Twinkle, Little Star")

Clouds, clouds in the sky.
Clouds, clouds way up high.
Some are white
And some are gray.
Slowly, slowly drift away.
Clouds, clouds in the sky.
Clouds, clouds way up high.

Kimberly Tynan, Clover Street School, Windsor, CT

Cloud in a Bag

Developing gross-motor skills: tossing and catching

Have each child crumple white paper shreds and place them in a small resealable plastic bag along with silver or iridescent shreds. Seal the bags and secure them with tape. Then have students use the resulting clouds to practice tossing and catching.

Rexann Roussel

Rain Cloud
Developing prewriting skills
Draw a large gray cloud on a piece of bulletin board paper and attach it to your wall. Provide crayons in several shades of blue. Show youngsters how to make dashed lines below the cloud so that the lines resemble rain. Then encourage little ones to visit the center to draw rain beneath the cloud. If desired, when the paper is full of raindrops, prompt youngsters to add black coloring to the cloud and yellow lightning zigzags beneath the cloud. Now it's a thunderstorm!

Tina Richards, Tina's Home Daycare, Shinnston, WV

Check This Out!
When Erin McGinness-Goldberg of Bear Early Education, Bear, Delaware, teaches a unit on clouds, she suspends cloud cutouts from her ceiling. Then she encourages youngsters to "fly" through the clouds when she transitions them to the next activity.

Reading in the Clouds
Developing an independent interest in books
To make a fluffy cloud-themed reading center, place a blue sheet or blanket on the floor. Cut cloud shapes from quilt batting and place them on the sheet. Then put white pillowcases on a variety of different pillows and arrange them in the center. Provide cloud-themed books, and this cozy reading center is in business!

Note to the teacher: Use with "Look Up!" on page 278.

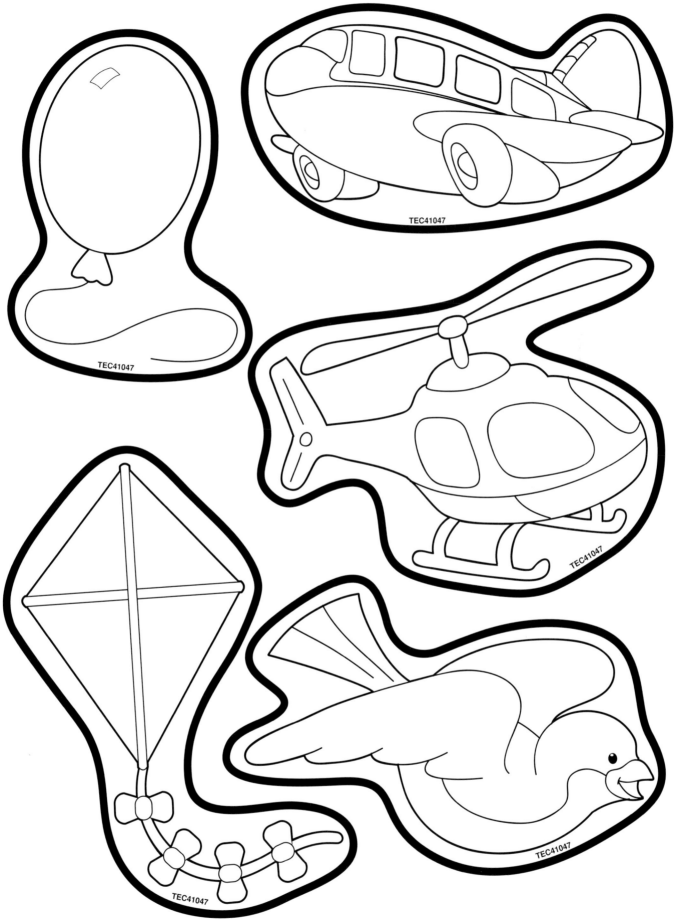

TEC41047

TEC41047

TEC41047

TEC41047

TEC41047

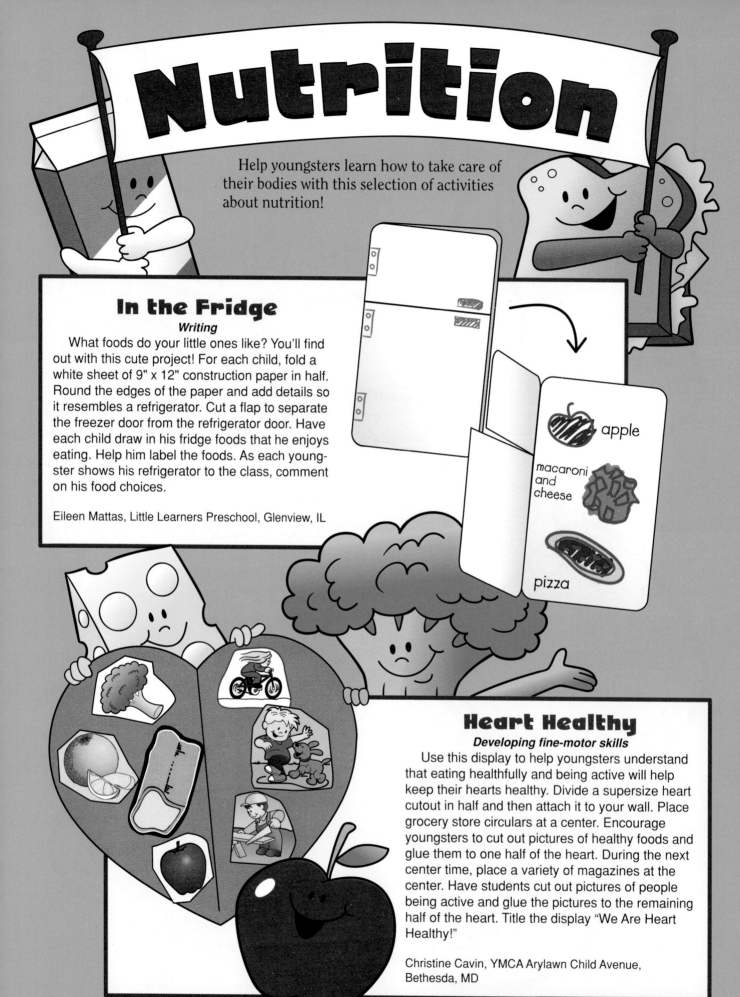

Nutrition

Help youngsters learn how to take care of their bodies with this selection of activities about nutrition!

In the Fridge
Writing
What foods do your little ones like? You'll find out with this cute project! For each child, fold a white sheet of 9" x 12" construction paper in half. Round the edges of the paper and add details so it resembles a refrigerator. Cut a flap to separate the freezer door from the refrigerator door. Have each child draw in his fridge foods that he enjoys eating. Help him label the foods. As each youngster shows his refrigerator to the class, comment on his food choices.

Eileen Mattas, Little Learners Preschool, Glenview, IL

apple

macaroni and cheese

pizza

Heart Healthy
Developing fine-motor skills
Use this display to help youngsters understand that eating healthfully and being active will help keep their hearts healthy. Divide a supersize heart cutout in half and then attach it to your wall. Place grocery store circulars at a center. Encourage youngsters to cut out pictures of healthy foods and glue them to one half of the heart. During the next center time, place a variety of magazines at the center. Have students cut out pictures of people being active and glue the pictures to the remaining half of the heart. Title the display "We Are Heart Healthy!"

Christine Cavin, YMCA Arylawn Child Avenue, Bethesda, MD

Grocery Guy
Recognizing healthy snacks

Encourage youngsters to try new healthy foods with Grocery Guy! Decorate a paper grocery bag as shown. Set Grocery Guy on the floor and place healthy food items in the bag to make a simple snack (see suggestions below). Introduce Grocery Guy to students, and tell them that he has brought some interesting foods. Have youngsters help prepare and then nibble on the snacks. Periodically throughout your nutrition unit, have Grocery Guy provide interesting new snacks.

Suggested snacks:
hummus and vegetables
lowfat yogurt and fruit
pita pockets filled with vegetables and low-fat dressing
bananas dipped first in yogurt and then in crushed cereal

Cindy Magrath, Lovell Weekday Ministry, Conway, SC

My Lunchbox
Participating in a song

Color and cut out a copy of the patterns on page 287. Ready the cutouts for flannelboard use. Then attach the cutouts to your board. Place a lunchbox nearby. Lead youngsters in singing the first two verses of the song. During the second verse, prompt a student to remove the sandwich and milk cutouts and place them in the lunchbox. Repeat the process with the remaining verse to fill the lunchbox with treats.

(sung to the tune of "London Bridge")

My lunchbox is full of treats,
Full of treats, full of treats.
My lunchbox is full of treats.
Mmmm-mmmm, yummy!

There's a sandwich and some milk,
And some milk, and some milk.
There's a sandwich and some milk.
Mmmm-mmmm, yummy!

There's some yogurt and some fruit,
And some fruit, and some fruit.
There's some yogurt and some fruit.
Mmmm-mmmm, yummy!

Cherie Durbin, Hickory, NC

Tossed Salad Collage

Expressing oneself through art

Make a copy of page 288 for each child. Explain that it's very important to eat a variety of colorful vegetables. Invite students to name several vegetables that a person might put in a salad. Then have little ones make their own salad collage. Direct each child to color the page. Then have her crumple pieces of light green tissue paper (lettuce) and attach them to the page. Encourage her to crumple and glue to the paper pieces of dark green tissue paper (green peppers), brown tissue paper (mushrooms), and orange tissue paper (carrots). Finally, have her glue red pom-poms (tomatoes) on the salad. What a tasty-looking collage!

adapted from an idea by Janeen Danielsen, Dike Discovery Center, Dike, IA

Splendid Salad

Did You Know?

You may be aware that apples are a good source of fiber and vitamin C, but did you know that eating an apple gives you an energy boost that may be a more reliable method of staying awake than drinking a cup of coffee? The natural sugar in the apple might be more effective than the caffeine in your morning cup of joe!

Time to Eat!

Participating in a rhyme

Lead youngsters in reciting the first couplet below. Then ask a child to name a healthy food such as yogurt or nonsugary cereal to have for breakfast. Guide students in reciting the second couplet, inserting the name of the food. Repeat the process several times. If desired, substitute "dinner" or "lunch" for "breakfast" and have students name appropriate foods.

Time for [breakfast]; time to eat.
What kind of food would be a healthy treat?

[Yogurt] for breakfast; time to eat.
[Yogurt] is a food that is a healthy treat.

Suzanne Moore, Tucson, AZ

TEC41047

TEC41047

MILK

YOGURT

TEC41047

TEC41047

Splendid Salad

Note to the teacher: Use with "Tossed Salad Collage" on page 286.

Let's Go to the ZOO

Your youngsters will be wild for these fabulous zoo-themed activities!

Z Is for Zoo
Forming the letter Z

This simple song and activity will earn a roar of approval from your little ones. Post a piece of bulletin board paper labeled with the word *Zoo*. Point out the word and explain that it begins with the letter *Z*. Lead youngsters in singing the song shown, encouraging students to draw the letter in the air during the fourth line. Then, during center time, encourage youngsters to draw and cut out pictures of zoo animals and glue the cutouts to the paper.

(sung to the tune of "I'm a Little Teapot")

I'm a little letter;
My name is *Z*.
You can draw me:
One, two, three!
You are sure to find me
At the zoo.
Zoo begins with *Z*—
It's true!

Marie E. Cecchini, West Dundee, IL

Cracker Count
Counting, comparing sets

Make two copies of the zoo mat on page 292. Place the mats at a table along with a supply of animal crackers, small cups, and a large die. Two youngsters visit the table, and each child takes a mat and a small cup of animal crackers. One child rolls the die and places that number of animal crackers on her mat. A second child repeats the process, placing crackers on his mat. The youngsters compare the numbers of zoo animals, using words such as *more, fewer,* and *the same.* They repeat the activity several times. Then they nibble on their crackers.

Phyllis Prestridge, West Amory Elementary, Amory, MS

Three Little Elephants

Participating in a rhyme

Elephants are always interesting zoo attractions. Celebrate these popular animals with a fun action rhyme!

Three big elephants—what a sight!
Swinging their trunks from left to right,
Flapping their ears, and stamping a beat
With their steady walking feet.
They might stop and trumpet at you
When you see them at the zoo.

Hold up three fingers.
Use arms to make a trunk.
Move hands to resemble ears and stamp feet.

Pause and then trumpet.
Point to eyes.

adapted from an idea by Crystal Jinkerson, Noah's Ark Preschool, Monroe, WI

Never, EVER Shout in a Zoo
by Karma Wilson Illustrated by Doug Cushman

When the little girl dropped her cone, she shouted. Then all the animals came out of the cages and took the keys. Then they locked up the people.

No Shouting!

Summarizing a story

A little girl drops her ice cream cone at the zoo, and she lets out a shout. That one shout leads to a chain of events that causes chaos in the zoo. With this three-dimensional project, youngsters summarize the events in *Never, Ever Shout in a Zoo* by Karma Wilson. In advance, mix equal parts of glue and non-mentholated shaving cream. Then tint the mixture with brown paint. Read the story aloud, encouraging youngsters to listen carefully to the events. Then have each child drop a blob of the mixture on a sheet of paper. Encourage her to place a construction paper cone in the mixture so it resembles the ice cream cone the little girl dropped. Finally, prompt each child to dictate a summary of the story.

What Will I See?

Writing

Cut out a copy of the booklet cover on page 293 for each child. Staple the cover atop four sheets of copy paper programmed with the sentence starter shown. Have each child draw on the first page a picture of an animal he would like to see at the zoo. Encourage him to use his own writing skills to complete the page with the animal's name. Then have him repeat the process for each remaining page.

What Might I See at the Zoo?
by Geoffrey

I might see
a Lion

Escaped Animals

Counting, developing vocabulary

Cut pictures of zoo animals from magazines. Place the animals around the room. Then lead youngsters in reciting the chant shown. Have little ones search for the animals and bring them back to your large-group area. Then prompt each student to name his animal. Encourage youngsters to place all the animals in a pile. Then help them count the animals aloud. How many animals escaped from the zoo?

Oh no! What should we do?
Some animals have escaped from the zoo!
Whether they're feathered or scaly or furry,
Gather those animals up in a hurry!

Jennie Jensen
North Cedar Elementary
Lowden, IA

Monkey-Tail Painting

Developing fine-motor skills

To make monkey tails, braid several strands of brown yarn. Secure the braids and then place them at a table along with shallow containers of paint. A child drags a monkey tail through the paint and then uses it to paint a sheet of paper. She continues with other monkey tails and paints until she is satisfied.

Crystal Jinkerson, Noah's Ark Preschool, Monroe, WI

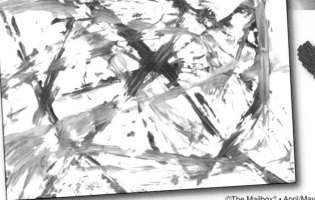

Welcome to the Zoo!

Note to the teacher: Use with "Cracker Count" on page 289.

What Might I See at the Zoo?

by _____

Note to the teacher: Use with "What Will I See?" on page 291.

THE MAILBOX **293**

Terrific Trees!

Little ones focus on trees with this lovely, leafy collection of activities!

ideas contributed by Roxanne LaBell Dearman
Western NC Early Intervention Program for Children Who
Are Deaf or Hard of Hearing
Charlotte, NC

Roots and Leaves
Identifying letters and letter sounds

Here's a "tree-mendously" fun activity that helps youngsters distinguish between two different letters. Display a simple, oversize tree drawing. Then place several *R* and *L* cards in a gift bag. Have a child choose a card and hold it up in the air. Encourage the remaining youngsters to identify the letter name. If the letter's sound is /l/ as in *leaf*, have the students put their arms in the air and wiggle their hands like leaves. If the letter's sound is /r/ as in *root*, have the students bend down and touch the floor. Then encourage the child to attach his card to the tree in the appropriate location.

Ring Rubbings
Developing fine-motor skills

In advance, use glue to draw concentric circles on tagboard circle cutouts so the tagboard resembles a cross-section of a tree. Then attach the cutouts to a tabletop. Place paper and unwrapped crayons by the cutouts. Then explain that when a tree is cut, there are several rings on the cut section. The number of rings tells the age of the tree. Invite youngsters to make rubbings of the cross-sections. Then encourage them to count the rings.

Beautiful Blooms
Developing one-to-one correspondence
Draw a large tree and place several dot stickers on the drawing so they resemble flower buds. Laminate the drawing and place it at a center along with flower-shaped cookie cutters and play dough. A youngster makes play dough flowers and places a flower over each bud. This tree will blossom right in front of his eyes!

Up High, Down Below
Participating in a song
This simple action song is sure to be popular with your little ones!

(sung to the tune of "The Farmer in the Dell")

The roots reach down below   *Touch your toes.*
To soak up water so   *Move hands up the body.*
That tree will grow and grow.   *Reach arms upward like branches.*
The roots reach down below.   *Touch your toes.*

The branches reach up high   *Reach arms upward like branches.*
So leaves can face the sky.   *Wiggle hands.*
To soak up light—that's why   *Arrange arms so they resemble the sun.*
The branches reach up high.   *Reach arms upward like branches.*

A dog, a little girl, a mom, and a fish all live in the tree.

A Silly Story
Creating a story innovation
Read aloud *Tree Ring Circus* by Adam Rex. In this story, a tree plays host to a variety of unique guests. As a follow-up to the story, have each child draw a large tree on a sheet of paper. Then encourage her to cut out magazine pictures and glue them to the tree. Encourage each child to describe what is in her tree as you write her words on the paper. If desired, bind youngsters' projects together into a class book.

Bare Tree, Pear Tree

Investigating living things

Give each child a copy of pages 297 and 298. Guide each student through the instructions shown to complete the booklet pages. When the pages are dry, have students add any desired details, such as leaves around the pears. Help each student cut apart her pages and assemble her booklet with a cover titled "Fabulous Fruit Tree." Then read the booklet aloud as she follows along.

Page 1: Color the page. Dip your pinkie finger in green paint and make prints along the branch so they resemble buds.

Page 2: Color the page. Crumple pieces of white facial tissue and glue them to the branch so they resemble flowers.

Page 3: Color the page. Dip your thumb in yellow paint and make prints so they resemble pears.

Page 4: Color the page.

Buds grow.

Blooms show.

2

Pears to share

Tree is bare.

4

Say It in Sign

Developing fine-motor skills

Encourage youngsters to use American Sign Language as they sing this adorable song celebrating trees!

(sung to the tune of "Are You Sleeping?")

I love trees; I love trees.

trees

Homes for birds; homes for bees.

birds

bees

Leaves up to the sky.

sky

Branches stretching high.

high

I love trees; I love trees.

trees

Buds grow.

1

©The Mailbox® • TEC41048 • April/May 2010

Blooms show.

2

There are pears to share.

3

The tree is bare.

4

Preschool Paradise!

Delight your little ones with this red-hot selection of tropical-themed activities!

Swishy Skirts

Developing fine-motor skills

Get youngsters properly outfitted for fine-motor (and gross-motor) fun with simple grass skirts! For each child, cut down the side of a paper grocery bag and cut away the bottom of the bag. (The bottom can be discarded or used for other crafts.) Wrap the bag around the child's waist and trim the bag so the edges do not quite meet. Next, have each child cut slits in the paper, as shown. (You may wish to mark a line across the top of the paper so youngsters know where to stop cutting.) When she is finished making slits, tape a length of yarn to the top of the resulting skirt as shown. Then wrap the skirt around her waist and tie it in place. Finally, play a selection of tropical music and encourage youngsters to move to the beat.

Amy Durrwachter, Kirkwood Early Childhood Center, Kirkwood, MO

Tropical Scents

Five senses: smell

Obtain several candles that have different tropical scents, such as banana, pineapple, coconut, passion fruit, or ocean breeze. Place them at a center and place a sheet of writing paper near each one. Then invite each youngster to smell each candle and identify her favorite scent. Prompt her to write her name on the paper near her favorite. After each youngster has voted, share the results with the class.

Shelley Hoster
Jack & Jill Early Learning Center
Norcross, GA

Lexi
Joel
Marianna
Ralpi

Chad
Jasmint

Tynell
Mikayla
Nick

Totally Tropical Fruit

Organizing data

Your little ones will be fascinated by these unique fruits! In advance, gather two different tropical fruits, such as kiwi and mango, and make a simple cutout of each fruit. Have youngsters observe and discuss the outside appearance of the fruits. Then invite each child to taste the fruits. Prompt her to decide which one she prefers. Then have her attach a clothespin to the appropriate cutout. Finally, help students count and compare each set of clothespins.

adapted from an idea by Shelley Hoster, Jack & Jill Early Learning Center, Norcross, GA

Ouch!

Participating in a song

This entertaining song is sure to cause oodles of giggles in your classroom!

(sung to the tune of "Three Blind Mice")

Coconuts, coconuts
Fall from the trees,
Fall from the trees.
I sat on the beach in my floppy hat.
They fell on my head—wasn't thinking that
I should have been wearing a big hard hat.
Coconuts, coconuts.

Debra Boudreau, First United Methodist Preschool and Kindergarten, Rocky Mount, NC

Paradise Play

Developing role-playing skills

Set up your dramatic-play area as a tropical paradise! Provide a suitcase with sun hats, sunglasses, visors, and Hawaiian shirts. Also provide beach towels, swim fins, goggles, play cameras, and empty sunscreen bottles. Your youngsters are sure to create a variety of tropical adventures with these props!

Marie E. Cecchini, West Dundee, IL
Roxanne LaBell Dearman, Western NC Early Intervention Program for Children Who Are Deaf or Hard of Hearing, Charlotte, NC

Tree Climbers
Investigating living things

Introduce little ones to animals that live in the tropics with this unique activity that uses text from the classic book *Chicka Chicka Boom Boom*! In advance, make a simple felt coconut tree and attach it to your flannelboard. Also color and cut out a copy of the animal patterns on pages 302 and 303 and ready them for flannelboard use. Have a child choose an animal. Help her identify the animal's name and place the animal on the tree. Then lead youngsters in reciting the chant shown, inserting the youngster's name and the animal's name. Continue in the same way with each remaining animal.

"Skit skat skoodle doot, flip flop flee!"
[Ava] put the [toucan] in the coconut tree!

Shelley Hoster, Jack & Jill Early Learning Center, Norcross, GA

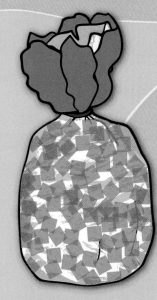

Pineapple Art
Developing fine-motor skills

This three-dimensional project is sweet! Help each youngster stuff a brown lunch bag with newspaper strips. Tie the bag closed and have the child paint it with a mixture of yellow paint and glue. While the mixture is still wet, encourage her to press brown tissue paper squares onto the project. Then have her tear green construction paper strips and press them on the top of the project. That looks good enough to eat!

Linda Hopkins, Patty Cakes Child Care Center, Oneida, NY

Paradise Water Bottles
Five senses: sight

Celebrate your paradise unit with these mini paradise bottles for youngsters to take home. Help each child pour blue-tinted water and vegetable oil in a small water bottle. Encourage him to sprinkle tropical-themed metallic confetti in the bottle. Then secure the cap with tape. Youngsters tilt and shake their bottles, watching the wavelike movement of the water and oil.

Danielle Lockwood, Colchester, CT

Animal Patterns
Use with "Tree Climbers" on page 301.

spider monkey

sloth

toucan

boa constrictor

tree frog

gecko

jaguar

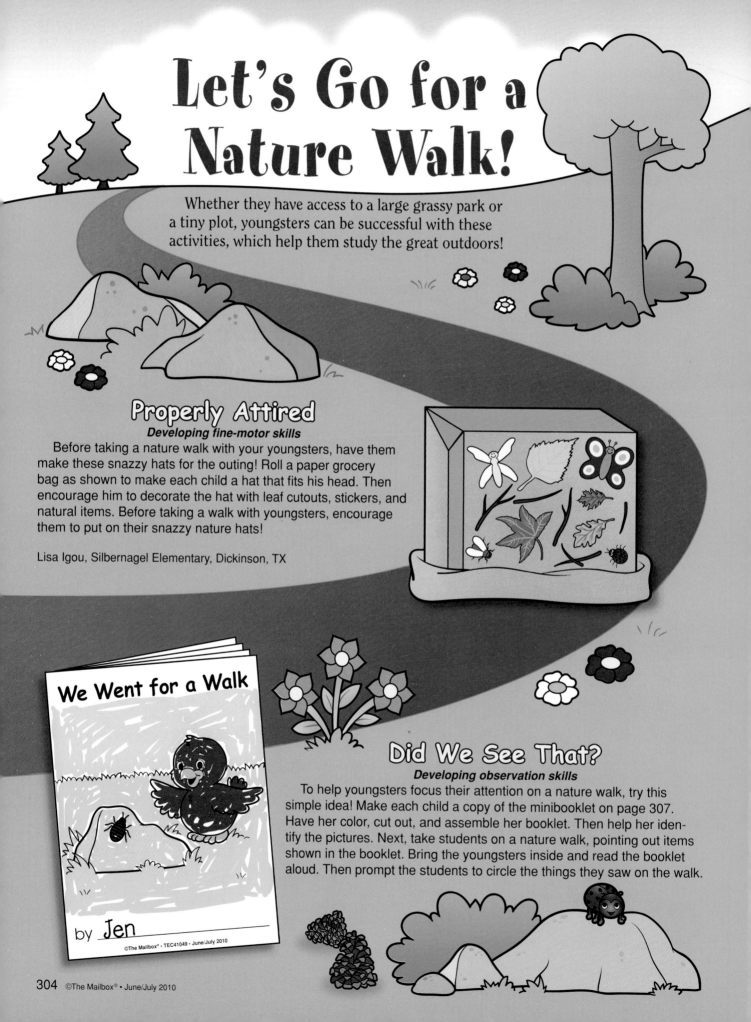

Let's Go for a Nature Walk!

Whether they have access to a large grassy park or a tiny plot, youngsters can be successful with these activities, which help them study the great outdoors!

Properly Attired
Developing fine-motor skills

Before taking a nature walk with your youngsters, have them make these snazzy hats for the outing! Roll a paper grocery bag as shown to make each child a hat that fits his head. Then encourage him to decorate the hat with leaf cutouts, stickers, and natural items. Before taking a walk with youngsters, encourage them to put on their snazzy nature hats!

Lisa Igou, Silbernagel Elementary, Dickinson, TX

We Went for a Walk

by Jen

Did We See That?
Developing observation skills

To help youngsters focus their attention on a nature walk, try this simple idea! Make each child a copy of the minibooklet on page 307. Have her color, cut out, and assemble her booklet. Then help her identify the pictures. Next, take students on a nature walk, pointing out items shown in the booklet. Bring the youngsters inside and read the booklet aloud. Then prompt the students to circle the things they saw on the walk.

Nature Collage

Comparing and contrasting

Have each youngster collect natural items in a lunch-size bag. Then, during center time, gather a small group of youngsters. For each child, remove the backing from a square of clear Con-Tact covering and place it on the table sticky-side up. Encourage each student to place his nature items on the sticky covering. Place a second sheet of Con-Tact covering over the first one. Then display these natural collages in your window, encouraging youngsters to notice the differences and similarities among the items each classmate found on the nature walk.

Marie E. Cecchini, West Dundee, IL

That Doesn't Belong!

Recognizing behaviors of a responsible citizen

While you are outdoors with your youngsters, don't forget to have them notice items that do not belong. While pointing out the birds, flowers, and grass, make note of any litter you see. When you find a piece of litter, lead students in singing the song below. Then pick up the item and make sure students see you place it in a trash can.

(sung to the tune of "If You're Happy and You Know It")

If you see some paper, wrappers, or a cup,
You should make sure that you try to pick them up.
Oh, I think you will agree;
Those aren't things we want to see.
Litter's ugly! If you can, please pick it up.

Shake your finger.
Place your hands on your hips.
Nod your head.
Shake your head.
Shake your finger.

adapted from an idea by Tami Manchester, Brick House School, Taunton, MA

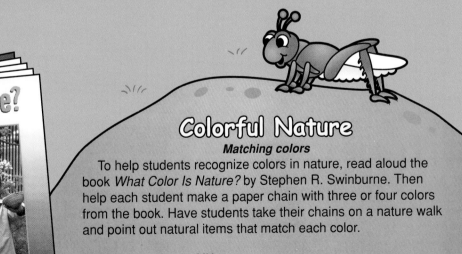

Colorful Nature

Matching colors

To help students recognize colors in nature, read aloud the book *What Color Is Nature?* by Stephen R. Swinburne. Then help each student make a paper chain with three or four colors from the book. Have students take their chains on a nature walk and point out natural items that match each color.

Terry Mattson, Austin, MN

A Nature Sit

Developing observational skills

When a nature walk isn't possible, try a nature sit! Use craft sticks and yarn to stake a 12-inch square of grass for each child. Then give each youngster a plastic magnifying glass, a clipboard, a sheet of paper, and a crayon. Encourage her to use her magnifying glass to observe the plot of grass. Then prompt her to draw and comment on the items she sees.

Ellie Brandel
Little Acorns Preschool, Milwaukie, OR

Check This Out!

To help youngsters keep their hands free while toting nature items, Ellen McNeil from Naval Submarine Base Child Development Center in Kings Bay, Georgia, gives each child a bracelet made from thick masking tape (sticky-side out). As a child finds natural items he would like to keep, he attaches them to his bracelet. Then he takes the bracelet home at the end of the day!

Press and Paint

Investigating living things

Encourage youngsters to collect (or bring from home) a variety of flowers, leaves, and grasses. Place the items in a mortar with a little bit of water and help students grind the items with a pestle. The water will change colors! Then have youngsters use the tinted water to make watercolor pictures.

Noel James, Greater Wenatchee Parent-Child Preschool
Wenatchee, WA

Editor's Tip:

If you don't have a mortar and pestle, weight a small soda bottle with rice and have students use it to grind the items in a plastic bowl with a little bit of water.

We Went for a Walk

by _____

©The Mailbox® • TEC41049 • June/July 2010

Did we see grass?

Did we see a bug?

3

Did we see a squirrel?

2

Did we see a tree?

Did we see a rock?

1

Did we see a bird?

Note to the teacher: Use with "Did We See That?" on page 304. To make the booklet, cut on the bold line. Fold along the thin horizontal line (keeping the programming to the outside) and then fold along the thin vertical line (keeping the cover to the outside).

Splendid Science Booklets

ideas contributed by Lucia Kemp Henry, Fallon, NV

What's Under My Feet?

What's under your youngsters' feet? They're sure to know when they make this cute booklet! Give each child a copy of pages 310 and 311. Encourage her to color the pages. Then guide her through the steps below to complete the booklet. Next, help her cut out the pages and staple them in order behind a cover labeled as shown.

Steps:

Page 1: Brush glue on the page. Sprinkle sand over the glue.

Page 2: Brush glue on the page. Sprinkle tiny rocks over the glue.

Page 3: Spread brown paint on the page. Sprinkle potting soil over the wet paint.

Page 4: Tear rock shapes from a brown paper grocery bag. Glue them to the page.

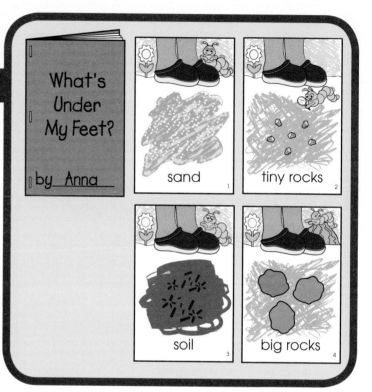

Up in the Sky

Give each child a construction paper copy of the booklet backing on page 312. Have him color the daytime sky blue and the nighttime sky black. Next, encourage him to sponge-paint a sun in the daytime sky and a moon in the nighttime sky. Label the paintings as shown. When the paint is dry, label three blue and three black 3" x 5" construction paper pages as shown. Stack the blue and black pages separately and staple each stack to the appropriate side of the backing. Then have each child attach cotton balls and star stickers to the appropriate pages.

Weather Through the Seasons

To make this adorable weather booklet, cut four 4½" x 6" blue construction paper pages and one 4½" x 6" construction paper cover for each child. Label the cover and pages with the words shown. Then guide each child through the steps below to complete each page. When the pages are finished, stack them with the cover on top and then staple them together.

Steps:

Page 1: Draw swirling lines on the page. Attach leaf cutouts and newspaper pieces.

Page 2: Dip your finger in white paint and then spread paint directly above the words. Make white fingerprints on the page. Sprinkle clear glitter over the wet paint.

Page 3: Squirt a line of blue paint directly above the words. Press a wide, dry paintbrush in the paint and then drag it up the page.

Page 4: Glue a yellow circle cutout to the page. Use white glue to make sun rays. Then sprinkle orange glitter over the glue.

My Five Senses

For each child, fold a 9" x 12" sheet of construction paper as shown and staple it to make a pocket. Cut five 4½" x 6" pages for each child. Label the cover and the pages as shown. Take and then print out a photo of each youngster holding up five fingers. Then have her attach her photo to her front cover. Help her follow the steps below to complete the pages. When the pages are finished, encourage her to tuck them in the pocket.

Steps:

Eyes: Attach colorful tissue paper scraps.

Ears: Attach a photocopy of a piece of music that is in the public domain.

Nose: Attach pictures of flowers from seed catalogs or magazines.

Mouth: Attach pictures of food cut from magazines.

Hands: Attach a soft piece of felt or fabric.

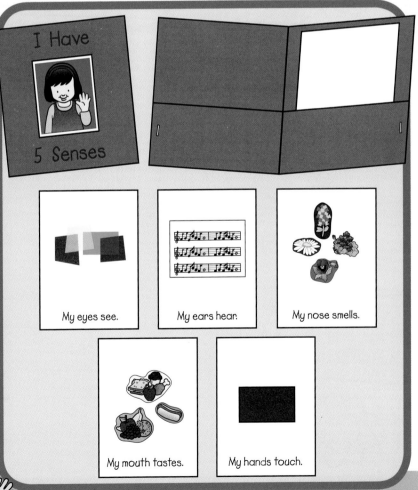

Booklet Pages 1 and 2

Use with "What's Under My Feet?" on page 308.

2

tiny rocks

1

sand

4

big rocks

©The Mailbox® • TEC41044 • Aug./Sept. 2009

3

soil

Booklet Backing
Use with "Up in the Sky" on page 308.

night

day

Index